PENGUIN BOOKS

MY FATHERS' DAUGHTER

Hannah Pool was born in Eritrea in 1974 and grew up in Manchester. Best known for her column 'The New Black', she is also a commissioning editor on the *Guardian Weekend* magazine. This is her first book.

Read more at www.hamishhamilton.co.uk

My Fathers' Daughter

HANNAH POOL

PENGUIN BOOKS

PENGUIN BOOKS

Published by the Penguin Group
Penguin Books Ltd, 80 Strand, London WC2R ORL, England
Penguin Group (USA) Inc., 375 Hudson Street, New York, New York 10014, USA
Penguin Group (Canada), 90 Eglinton Avenue East, Suite 700, Toronto, Ontario, Canada M4P 2Y3
(a division of Pearson Penguin Canada Inc.)
Penguin Ireland, 25 St Stephen's Green, Dublin 2, Ireland
(a division of Penguin Books Ltd)
Penguin Group (Australia), 250 Camberwell Road, Camberwell, Victoria 3124, Australia
(a division of Pearson Australia Group Pty Ltd)
Penguin Books India Pvt Ltd, 11 Community Centre, Panchsheel Park, New Delhi – 110 017, India
Penguin Group (NZ), cnr Airborne and Rosedale Roads, Albany, Auckland 1310, New Zealand
(a division of Pearson New Zealand Ltd)
Penguin Books (South Africa) (Pty) Ltd, 24 Sturdee Avenue, Rosebank, Johannesburg 2196, South Africa

Penguin Books Ltd, Registered Offices: 80 Strand, London WC2R ORL, England

www.penguin.com

First published by Hamish Hamilton 2005
Published in Penguin Books 2006
1

Set by Rowland Phototypesetting Ltd, Bury St Edmunds, Suffolk
Printed in England by Clays Ltd, St Ives plc

ISBN-13: 978-0-141-01604-7
ISBN-10: 0-141-01604-3

for David

Acknowledgements

I could not have got through the last two years or so, never mind written this book, without the help and support of others, to all of whom I owe a huge debt of gratitude. Thank you to my early and very loyal readers, Emma Brockes and Gary Younge, who made me feel like I wasn't doing this on my own, for which I will be eternally grateful. Thanks to Kari Greaves and Graham Parry for their kindness and generosity, and thanks to Katharine Viner of the *Guardian*, for having faith in me from the beginning. Thanks also to Hannah Griffiths for helping me get started, and to Vivienne Schuster at Curtis Brown and Simon Prosser and Juliette Mitchell at Penguin for keeping me going with their wonderful encouragement, patience and advice. Thanks to those who helped me find my feet in Eritrea, and those who kept me sane upon my return: Jennifer Walters, Lucy Manning, Debra Tammer, Lemn Sissay, and many others – if you're wondering whether or not I mean you then I probably do. And finally, thanks to Gaim Kibreab for welcoming me into the family.

Eritrean Family Tree

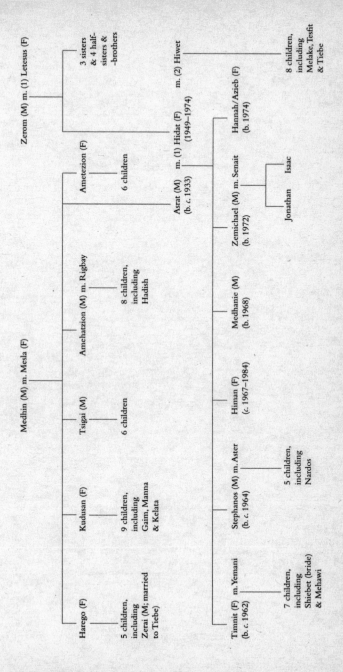

I

What do you wear to meet your father for the first time? It's 5.30 p.m. local time. I am in a room in the Ambasoira Hotel, in the centre of Asmara, the capital of Eritrea. I arrived three days ago, after nearly thirty years of waiting. I left this place when I was six months old and have not returned until now. My cousin Manna has just called to say he will be here to pick me up in a taxi in ten minutes' time. From the Ambasoira we will drive through the centre of Asmara, along the palm-tree-lined Liberation Avenue, and across town to the area of Mai Tameni. Waiting for me in Mai Tameni are my father, three brothers and a sister, none of whom I have ever met. Some women plan their wedding day from the moment they are old enough to draw a white dress. I have always planned this moment.

The first step to finding my birth family was telling my dad I was planning to go to Eritrea. Tracing my birth family felt like the most disloyal thing I could do. I hate it when people call my dad my 'adoptive' dad, it feels like they are dismissing him, relegating him to second best, but telling him I wanted to trace was like the ultimate betrayal: 'Thanks for choosing me, thanks for looking after me for the last thirty years, but I've decided that my life just isn't complete until I meet the people that couldn't even be bothered to keep me.' That's what telling him felt like.

The tracing dilemma goes to the heart of what it means to

be adopted. Questions of blood and identity, of what makes someone family and what it means to be a parent, or a child, all come to a head when tracing is brought into an already heady mix. If my birth father is still alive, whose child am I?

So here's the scenario: you tell your parents you want to trace; they take it badly, your relationship is ruined; you then go and find your birth parents, they don't want to know – and bingo, you're back where you started, parentless, only you're too old for an orphanage. That's why so many adoptees trace in secret. Not because we're naturally sneaky or manipulative, not because we're 'ungrateful little shits' (what one friend was called when she told her mother she wanted to trace) but because we live in fear of rocking the parental boat.

But not telling my dad was never really an option, partly due to the circumstances of my particular situation. I was born in 1974, in a *hidmo* (a large hut) in a village outside Keren, Eritrea. To those who have never heard of it, I describe Eritrea as running along the coast of the Horn of Africa, looking out across the Red Sea, and sharing borders with Ethiopia, Sudan, and Djibouti. Eritrea is roughly the same size as the UK, but with a population of just 3.5 million (roughly that of Manchester). Even by African standards Eritrea has not had an easy time of it. From the sixteenth century, when it was part of the Ottoman empire, to the nineteenth-century 'Scramble for Africa', when Eritrea became an Italian colony, this small country has constantly had to fight for its right to exist. Everyone wants a piece of it. The piece they want in particular tends to be Massawa, the port once known as the 'Pearl of the Red Sea', which has been held variously by the Portuguese, Arabs and Egyptians, as well as the Turks, British, Italians and, of course, the Ethiopians.

I say 'and of course' the Ethiopians because that's the reply I tend to get when I tell people where I'm from – 'Ah yes, isn't Eritrea part of Ethiopia?' Hardly. At the last count approximately 80,000 people have died in the struggle for Eritrea's independence from Ethiopia, a battle that, lasting over thirty years and with flare-ups as recently as 2000, holds the dubious honour of being Africa's longest war.

In 1941, after nearly half a century of Italian rule, the British took control of Eritrea, as occupied enemy territory, until 1952, when, courtesy of the UN, Eritrea was federated with Ethiopia under the sovereignty of the Emperor of Ethiopia, Haile Selassie. Soon after, Eritrean leaders were booted out of office, Amharic (Ethiopian) replaced Tigrinya (Eritrean) and Arabic as the official language and, as a final insult to the country's people, in 1962 Eritrea was annexed and became a province of Ethiopia. The country had been swallowed up completely and no longer existed on maps of Africa. By the early 1960s, after years of being ignored by the international community, Eritrean resistance to Ethiopian rule ('the Struggle') had well and truly begun. It was a wholly uneven battle. Eritrea's tiny guerrilla force against Ethiopia's comparatively massive army, which was funded by two superpowers (the Americans and then the Russians). The war, and the famine and poverty that came with it, emptied the country (a third of the population is living in exile) and filled the orphanages. Finally, in 1991, the EPLF (Eritrean People's Liberation Front) took Asmara, and Eritrea won its independence.

In 1974 my dad was teaching politics at Sudan's nearby University of Khartoum. His wife Marya was doing voluntary work with Catholic nuns, also in Khartoum. The nuns told Marya about the orphanage in Eritrea and she decided to pay a visit. She left with me. Long before the images of Romanian orphanages started a trend, long before the Chinese baby girl scandals in the tabloids, long before it was fashionable, I was adopted because my parents 'wanted to make a difference'. The orphanage told Marya I had no family: my mother had died in childbirth, my father not long after. I weighed two and a half kilos, was malnourished and covered in chicken pox. If she did not take me, the orphanage said, I'd probably be dead in six months.

I went with her to Khartoum; she guessed I was about six months old.

Four years later, Marya, a loving but deeply depressed woman, took an overdose. My dad wanted to return to England, but was anxious about taking a young child there while he didn't have any means of support. It was decided I should go to stay with family friends while my dad sorted himself out. Nothing strange there then. Apart from the fact that these friends lived in Norway.

A few months in Norway turned into a couple of years, due to the combined bureaucracy of immigration and inter-country adoption. By the time my dad came to get me, I was fluent in Norwegian. Only. I have plenty of memories from Norway – sledging in the winter, picnics in the summer. To this day, I take childish pride in the fact that the Norwegian national day is near to my own birthday.

'The Norway years', as I call them, are something of a red herring in my life. Though happy, my memories run like a silent film. Hardly surprising really, as I can't speak Norwegian any more – there wasn't much call for it in Manchester. After what seemed like an eternity, my dad came to get me from Stavanger, the small Norwegian port where I was living. I went from there to Manchester. I have no idea how I coped. My oldest school friend remembers me not speaking English ('We just thought you were speaking some weird African language'). To me the memory is less clear; it's more a general feeling of confusion that accompanies a lot of my early school memories.

My dad was now a lecturer in government at Manchester University, and Eritrea was one of his areas of expertise. The next decade or so was blissfully 'normal': my dad remarried, he and his wife had two children, I picked up a Manchester accent. All the while, I studiously ignored any attempts my dad made at trying to teach me about my heritage. 'I'm not Eritrean, I'm just black' was my favourite line.

Then came 1991, and Eritrean liberation. On 24 May 1993 independence was declared (after a referendum in which 99.81 per cent voted in favour). The guerrilla fighters my dad got to know in the 1970s were now ministers in the post-liberation government. My dad, along with many other long-term supporters of the Struggle, was invited by the new regime to the celebrations. During the trip, on a whim, he decided to visit the orphanage. An English priest, who also happened to be paying a visit, accompanied him. To my dad's surprise, the orphanage was still there, as was Sister Gabriella, the nun who'd arranged my adoption. After a chat and a tour of the orphanage, my dad left, leaving Sister Gabriella with a recent photograph of me for old times' sake, and thinking no more of it.

Months later, back in Manchester, the priest got in touch with my father. The nun had spoken to him after my dad had left – you could call it a confession. I wasn't an orphan. Not only was my father alive, but I had at least one older brother,

5

who it seemed had been brought up in the orphanage. A few months later another letter came from the priest: this time, with a letter enclosed from my older brother.

This letter has taken on almost mystical properties. I've read it so often, looking for clues, for answers. For some sense of who they are. For a sense of who I am. When I first received the letter it was so powerful, so charged, I couldn't read it without breaking down. My dad gave it me when I was back in Manchester during a break from my studies at Liverpool University where I was finishing a sociology degree. Back in Liverpool, alone with the explosive letter, I felt completely at sea. What was I supposed to do? Was I supposed to reply? How? What do you say to a brother you've never met? To a brother who, by the sound of things, got 'left behind'. To a brother whose mother died giving birth to a sister who was whisked off to a life of relative ease. While I was getting to grips with fast food, rah-rah skirts and Enid Blyton, they were coping with war, famine and drought.

And yet he was my brother and I felt overwhelmed at the thought of someone who shared my genes. There was a gulf between us but, ultimately, we had the same parents, we were from the same place. If we met, would there be a connection, an invisible bond because we were brother and sister? Would we smile the same, laugh the same, cry the same? Or was this man, connected to me only by blood, no more than a stranger?

I already had a brother in Manchester, who I'd known every day of his life. I might not share genes with Tom, but I couldn't love him more. I shared a history with him. I was his sister. I didn't just feel proud of his achievements; I felt envy and relief that I had a fourteen-year head start. Surely that proved our credentials as siblings.

One was white and English, the other was black and Eritrean, but which one was my true brother?

To my shame, the only way I could deal with the letter was to ignore it. I hid it away, reading it only occasionally, when I was alone and sure I wouldn't disturb anyone with my crying. It moved with me, from house to house, in a box full of keepsakes. I'd go for months without taking it out, worried that if I did I wouldn't be able to put it back again. I decided that I should probably concentrate on my degree, and then deal with the letter afterwards. Degree completed, I reasoned it was probably best if I didn't act on the letter until I'd finished my postgraduate course. Postgraduate course finished, I thought I should probably focus all my energy on getting a job. After all, what would have been the point of all that waiting if I then went and blew it by not getting a decent job? I might as well have 'dealt' with the letter as soon as I'd received it, in that case.

Incidentally, my excuses weren't always career-oriented. Depending on my circumstances, I'd regularly swing from deciding I should wait until I had the support of a stable relationship, to thinking this was a mission best accomplished when I was single, without the distractions of a boyfriend. Dealing with the letter, like the letter itself, became an almost abstract idea. By 'dealing with it', I knew I meant tracing my birth family, and after that, I just didn't know. Never mind a can of worms, this felt more like I was teetering on the edge of an abyss. Once I went over, there would be no going back, but boy what a ride it would be if I made it to the other side. And just imagine how I'd feel if I lived to tell the tale!

My birth family had tried to contact me and I had ignored them. I thought I was 'just waiting', but I now realize that by doing nothing, I was effectively making a decision. But doing nothing is not the easy way out I thought it was. I don't know if it was that I'd run out of excuses, or that I'd stopped making them. But over the last twelve months things had changed, and doing nothing was no longer an option. My main fear had shifted from 'What if they reject me?' to 'What if I've left it too late?' The letter, written nine years ago, might have frozen them in my mind, but their lives would have moved on. I had to face the very real possibility that, assuming he was alive at the time of the letter, my birth father might have died during the time it had taken for me to get my head around his existence. The big difference was that it was a risk I was now willing to take. In fact it was a risk which was highly preferable to the alternative: a lifetime of wondering, what if?

So I set the ball rolling. I told my dad I wanted to trace. There must have been something in the air, because my dad then told me that Fessehaie, an Eritrean friend of his in London, had called him a couple of weeks before saying that he had been contacted by a friend and relative of his wife Wozenet, who talked about how his family had a 'missing' daughter, thought to have been adopted from the Asmara orphanage by an English academic. My dad gave me Fessehaie's number and I called him up and arranged to visit him at home, in Finsbury Park, north London. Five days later, I was in Fessehaie's sitting room, being told I had a cousin in London. I left in a state of shock, having arranged, through Fessehaie, to meet my cousin at Chiswick tube station the following Sunday.

2

It's been such a long week. I haven't been able to get my cousin out of my head. Just calling him 'my cousin' seems odd. I've told a couple of friends about the meeting on Sunday and each time I hear myself say the words 'my cousin', it's something of a shock. The words got stuck halfway and more times than not I ended up referring to him as 'my sort-of cousin'.

'What do you mean "sort-of"?'

'Um . . .'

'Is his mother your father's sister?'

'Well, yes.'

'Then he's your cousin, there's no sort-of about it.'

'I suppose so,' I'd say, bewildered every time. It just doesn't feel real. I think it's the fact he's in London as much as anything else. All this while, I've had a cousin in London. If only I'd known, maybe things would have been different. All those times I felt on my own. All those times when it might have been nice to have a family member around – not just at the end of the phone. Maybe I wouldn't have had to move so many times, or crash on so many people's floors when I was in between rented flats. Or when relationships broke up and I found myself homeless once again. Maybe I wouldn't have made such rushed choices, been so quick to move in with boyfriends, if I'd had the safety net of family in London. Then again, I think, maybe if things had been easier, I might not have been so determined to buy my own place, to make London welcome me, to make it my home no matter what.

I've had to stop myself calling him and asking if we can bring the meeting forward. Twice I got as far as dialling his number – only from work, mind, so he couldn't do 1471. I don't want him to think I'm a stalker or anything.

By Wednesday, I hit on the idea of Googling him. A timetable of an academic conference in Sweden came up, and he was on it. There was an option to look at a photograph of him giving a talk, but something stopped me. Looking at him before the meeting felt like cheating. So I closed down the link and tried to get on with my work.

That evening when I got home I wanted to call him again. It took all my will-power not to, so I made a deal with myself – if I didn't call, I could look at the picture the next day.

The next morning, Thursday, I sat hunched over my screen weighing up my options. Opening the picture might ruin the moment we met, take away the element of surprise, but by not opening it I risked losing my cool and just calling the guy up, thereby coming across like some needy girlfriend, and scaring him off. Surely, then, by opening the picture I'd be doing him and myself a favour? Right, that settled it, it was either open the picture and don't call, or don't open the picture and call.

As soon as I clicked on to the picture option I wished I hadn't. I was overcome with guilt, like I'd broken my side of a bargain or found a Christmas present early – the ecstasy of discovering you have got what you wanted is quickly turned sour by the guilt of the fact you've broken an unwritten rule by looking for it in the first place. But it was too late now – I'd got the guilt, so I might as well look at the damn thing.

It was a rubbish picture. It looked like it'd been taken with a disposable camera from the worst seat at the very back of a very large lecture hall. The subject, my cousin, was standing behind a podium, head bent, reading from notes. All you could see, other than the vast expanse of lecture hall, was the top of his head. I smiled at the sight of his Afro. Well, at least we had a hairstyle in common. I tried to enlarge the image but to no effect. Afro aside, the picture had given me nothing. It had taken me the best part of a week to build up to looking at it, and I might as well not have bothered. All that 'should I, shouldn't I?' stuff was a complete waste of time and energy.

So why was I so pleased? Actually, it was more like relief – I didn't have the will-power to resist the picture, but I was chuffed it was so bad. It felt like I was tempted with the forbidden fruit, but unlike poor old Eve, I got away with it. If I sneaked off quietly, then no one would ever know I broke my part of the deal. All I had to do was keep it together and not go looking for any more clues.

I've done it. The relief I felt at learning precisely nothing from the photograph has kept my hands from the telephone for the rest of the week. I've made it to Sunday, and today I will meet my first ever blood relative. And not just some distant, third cousin once removed, but an actual cousin – my father is his mother's brother. It's a clear March day, and I've got an hour before I leave my flat to go and meet my cousin. I feel like I'm getting ready for a blind date. The floor of my flat is completely covered with clothes. What on earth should I wear? I want to look smart, like I've done OK in life, but not too pleased with myself. Anything too cool or painfully fashionable is out. Skirt or trousers? Are my favourite jeans too tight? One man's fitted is another's tarty, but then again I don't want to look too casual, like I couldn't be bothered to make an effort.

OK, if I treat it as a first date, then at least I'm on home turf. What image do I want to put across? That's easy – I want to look like the perfect long-lost cousin. If he is even half as nervous as I am about this, then he'll have been thinking about this moment for years, he'll have built up a mental image of me, so all I have to do is figure out what that mental image is, and dress accordingly. Christ, there isn't even anyone I can call for advice; it's not as if *Vogue* ever ran a feature on how to dress for this occasion, next to how to do vintage or whatever.

After trying on pretty much everything I own, I realize I have nothing appropriate. If I hadn't spent the best part of last week agonizing over a grainy photograph, I'd have figured this out by now, or at least had time to go shopping. As it is, I'll have to settle for jeans (casual, not too scary, etc.) with a plain black top (long-sleeved and loose to make up for tightness of the jeans) and heels to smarten the whole thing up. Classic, rather than trendy, and as long as my g-string doesn't pop out I should be able to carry the whole thing off.

Now that I'm dressed, I wish I wasn't. Panicking over what to wear was a pleasing distraction – it kept the reality of what I'm about to do at bay. Questions are flying around my head, with no seeming order, but at an alarming speed. Will he be angry with me for leaving it so long? Will he know if my father is alive? Will he have a message from him or a photograph? Will he recognize me straight away? Did he know my mother? Do I look like her?

I feel physically sick at the prospect of having these questions answered. You know what they say about wishing too hard for something? Well, that doesn't even come close. Try abject terror. Terror you can feel in the pit of your stomach, like you've swallowed it whole, like it's growing minute by minute and unless you do something about it, get rid of it somehow, then it's going to consume you, paralysing you for ever. For the first time all week I start to contemplate not going. I could call him and tell him I'm not well. Or perhaps get a friend to call for me. Yeah, that'd look like I was really sick, and not just bailing out. That's what I'll do, and I'll get them to tell him I'll call him when I'm better, but they don't know when that'll be, probably in a week or so. That's genius: not only do I get out of this ridiculous blind date, but it also buys me a bit of time. I'd feel bad involving someone else, though. Plus I'd have to tell them the whole story, and then they might talk me round, thinking they're doing me a favour.

I could just not show up – that's pretty simple, and doesn't need anyone else. I just won't show up, and when he calls wondering where I am, I'll pretend I thought it was next weekend, and that unfortunately I'm busy all week but shall we make it next weekend as the date is already in my diary? That's pretty good – I'll just sound suitably apologetic but also very keen, then I can go to the pub and just chill out, instead of having to traipse across London to meet a complete stranger who'll probably spend the whole time having a go at me anyway. It does mean I'll have to leave him standing at the tube station for a while until he realizes I'm not coming, which I feel a bit bad about, but he won't be there more than half an hour, and that's pretty much how long it'll take me to get there next week, so we'll be even. I suppose if I don't want to waste his time, I could call now and pretend I've got an emergency, or have to go to work, then at least he won't be cross with me next week for messing him around. But that involves speaking to him and if I have to speak to him, well, I might as well go. I wonder how long it'd take him to get to the tube station. I could call his house when I know he'll have left, to tell him about my emergency. That way it looks like I've tried to do the right thing by letting him know, not wanted to waste his time – it's just really unfortunate I can't make it, and if I say it's a 'work thing' that makes me sound responsible; or if it's a friend's emergency I'll sound caring and selfless. Either way, I can't go wrong.

Great. Now I've given myself a headache. Maybe I'm coming down with something? If I call him now and tell him I'm ill he'll never believe me. Shit, what if he's left his house already? I've got no mobile number for him, so he'll just be stood there waiting for me, thinking I've stood him up, getting angrier and angrier by the minute. Thinking, 'Well, what do you expect from someone who takes ten years to make contact with her family?'

I neck a couple of painkillers, just to take the edge off, and try to figure out how much time I've got left: thirty minutes, and even then I'll probably be early.

I put the CD player on – 'Greatest Day', a euphoric track by British soul diva Beverley Knight, comes on, definitely a good omen – and pick the discarded clothes up from the floor. The CD skips, which is definitely a bad omen, so I try the next track, 'Made it Back', willing it to play. It does – phew, I'm back on course – and I carry on tidying. Annoyingly, this only takes about five minutes. I look around and realize the place is pretty much immaculate. In various states of tension this week, I have hoovered, washed up, cleaned the bath and taken out the rubbish, twice. There are no decent displacement activities left. So I paint my nails. I opt for a calming baby pink – girlie, but not too tarty, I hope.

Finally, it's time to leave the flat. As I lock up, it occurs to me that when I next turn the keys in my front door I'll know if my father is alive.

I decide to walk to the tube stop, rather than wait for a bus, hoping the walk will calm me. But as I walk up Roman Road in the March sunshine I'm not especially calm – in fact I feel like I could break into a run at any minute. What would calm me down? A cigarette, that's what.

I've smoked on and off since I was fourteen, and like a true addict, I think I'm ambivalent about it. I've quit several times, once for two years, and more recently for ten months. But at this particular moment the only thing I can think would calm me down is a cigarette. But I know the routine. One cigarette usually leads to me finishing the packet (shame to waste it), which leads me to another, and so it goes for the next few months, until something inside me stirs and I realize how stupid I'm being, and stop all over again.

But this is different. It's not exactly a situation I'll find myself in again, so it doesn't matter if I have just one, if I ease the journey with a little smoke. Surely anything that will make today a bit easier is a good thing? I'm just about to go into a newsagent when a thought occurs to me. If I have a cigarette I'll smell of smoke, and Fag Ash Cousin is not really the impression I'm after. Damn. The cigarette is definitely out: he could smell it on me and then report back to my father that I smoke, and I definitely don't want my father knowing I smoke. I'm not sure why – after all it's not as if he was ever there to tell me about the evils of tobacco – but, well, I don't know, he might blame my dad or something, and that's not on. So no calming cigarette for me.

On the tube, I wonder if I should make a list of questions, just in case my mind goes blank. I'd toyed with the idea of bringing a tape recorder but dismissed it, as I thought it might look a bit, well, odd – accusatory even: 'Hi, I'm your long-lost cousin, now for the tape can you please make an audible response?' I rummage in my bag and realize my work note-book is at the bottom, and feel instantly comforted. For all I know, this might be our first and only meeting, and if I'm too overwhelmed to remember anything it could be gone, for ever. I haven't waited all this time only to forget each detail as a new one is revealed.

On the top of a clean sheet, I write, 'Is my father still alive?' But then I scribble it out again – it's not exactly a soft opener. 'Why was I put in the orphanage?' isn't much better. Perhaps I should ask him something about himself first, like his age, or how long he's been living in London. That's much more first-date material.

The knot in my stomach is back and the band around my head is tighter. I should have had that cigarette, and a drink wouldn't go amiss either. Damn, why didn't I have a glass of wine or something before I came out? That would have been the sensible thing to do. At this rate, assuming I make it to Chiswick heart-attack free, I'll be so jittery he'll run a mile. Hardly a good advert for a Western upbringing. If I'm early I'll find a bar and have a cigarette (just one) and a glass of red wine. Then later, I'll fess up to having a drink, and he'll just think the reason I smell like an ashtray is because I've been sitting in a bar. The only flaw is that this means he'll probably put me down for a bit of a drinker; but still it's better than him knowing I smoke, which I don't anyway, not really. I'm sitting on a rickety underground train. The journey is twenty-four stops on the District Line – that's pretty much the length of the entire line.

The last seven days have been unbearably long and frighteningly short at the same time. I've waited for this moment – to meet a member of my own family, a blood relative – all my life, but I don't feel ready for it. I wish I could fast forward the next couple of hours, then, depending on how it has gone, erase it or play it back on a loop.

I should have worn a skirt. Skirts are much classier. What possessed me to wear a pair of skintight jeans? I've definitely been in London too long.

Before I know it, we're at Chiswick. I jump out in a rush. I'm fifty minutes early, thank goodness: plenty of time for a drink and a cigarette. I nip into a newsagent next door to the tube and buy ten Camel Lights, a box of matches and some gum (genius). Thirty seconds later, I'm at the bar of a pub called the Tabard, ordering a glass of house red, 'Large, please'. The pub has the exterior of a traditional boozer, but the inside – all wood floors and church pews – has been well and truly gentrified. I sit down on a hard pew and take a long sip of the wine before unwrapping the cellophane on the cigarette packet. I pull the first cigarette I touch out of the packet and turn it upside down, before returning it to the packet. If ever there was a moment I needed a lucky cigarette it's now. I take another from the pack and as I go to light it I realize I'm shaking. The fact I'm shaking, rather than the action itself, is bewildering. I stare down at my right hand, cigarette between forefinger and middle finger, as if it belongs to someone else. When was the last time I shook with fear?

Jesus, I'm screwed if this cigarette and booze plan doesn't work. Not only will I smell of alcohol and nicotine, but I'll have the shakes too. Perfect. Might as well shoot some smack in front of him while I'm at it. I cast my gaze around the pub. Wouldn't it be funny if he was in here, having a secret cigarette and a drink to calm his nerves?

Ah, that was nearly a joke, that's a good sign – I'm obviously feeling calmer. Thank goodness. I was freaking myself out a bit there on the train with all those questions and then the shaking malarkey. I inhale deeply and think about nothing but watching the smoke leave my body. Relaxing into it, I take another sip of wine. The warmth of the liquid rises up, relaxing me further. The routine – drag, sip, relax; drag, sip, relax – is both calming and distracting. I congratulate myself on coming so early.

The people on the next table are deep in the midst of an intense discussion about football. Disjointed titbits of the conversation float over. 'You're mid Division One, and that's that.' It's nice to know life, and football, carries on.

A few minutes pass by, and I notice with mild amusement that I'm feeling rather light-headed. I try to figure out which has gone to my head, the cigarette or the wine. I haven't eaten since breakfast and as it's now nearly 5.30, it's probably the wine. I don't have another cigarette, one really was just enough, but it's nice to know they are there, in the zip-up part of my bag so they don't accidentally spill out. I pop a piece of gum into my mouth and instinctively reach for my lip balm and gloss and apply them for the third time since leaving the house. I should probably leave now. I'll just give the gum a chance to kick in. I can't very well walk up there chewing away, can I?

Is it better to be a few minutes early, or a few minutes late? Early could look a little keen, desperate even. I'd never be early for a date, and even if I was early I'd walk around the block or something. Then again, I'd also never be more than a couple of minutes late – after all if someone has gone to the effort of arranging to meet you, the least you can do is be there when you say you will. I decide on two minutes past – not too keen, but at the same time not rude or disrespectful.

What's that God-awful noise? Up on the television the England rugby team is singing 'God Save the Queen', which is a pretty good cue to leave the premises. I ditch the gum in the ashtray, next to the cigarette stub, and stand up to leave.

I walk into the tube station and glance around. I could probably still do a runner. Just hop back on to the tube and forget all about it. Leave things pretty much as they were. Maybe it's better that way, it's not like I'll miss what I never had.

3

'Hannah?' says a deep voice to my left. I turn and come face to face with a tall man, whose skin is exactly the same colour and tone as mine. Instantly ditching any plans of doing a runner, I smile and hold out my hand. 'Gaim?'

He is about forty to forty-five, tall and thin with delicate features and an air of elegance that comes with height, and of course the Afro that I recognize from the picture on the website.

'It is wonderful to meet you,' says Gaim, kissing me not once, or twice, but three times on the cheek. After the third kiss, he steps back, patting both of my shoulders, looks me dead on and says, 'My, how you look like your mother.'

Unsure how to respond, I just smile meekly, swallowing the lump in my throat.

'Shall we find somewhere quiet to sit and chat?' says Gaim, taking my hand and leading me out of the tube station. If he is stunned he isn't showing it, but then perhaps I am stunned enough for the both of us.

We walk in silence for a few minutes, neither of us knowing where to begin. Eventually, still reeling from the comment about my mother, I decide to take refuge in small talk. 'So have you lived around here for long?' I ask.

We chat about London, the traffic, the weather – typically safe first-date topics. We find a café and take a seat in the window. At least we can people-watch if the conversation dries up. As the waitress takes our order I wish we could just stay at that moment. Not get beyond small talk. He orders coffee, I order a beer. Then, as the waitress turns to leave us, I want to shout after her, 'Don't go, don't leave me here with this man, don't you see how dangerous he could be? He could be about to ruin the rest of my life!' But she's gone.

Gaim and I turn to face each other. He smiles. I grin back like a demented TV breakfast presenter. If I show enough teeth it might distract from the panic in my eyes.

'I was worried we might miss each other,' I lie. A good start, lying already. I was worried about a million things, but never that. If anything, I had assumed we'd just sort of know.

'You're a carbon copy of your mother.'

Round one to him then.

'I'd know you anywhere. Your face, your features, your size, everything.'

'My size? But you're really tall – how come?' I hear myself ask.

Christ, that's my first question? I've waited for the best part of three decades to meet a blood relative, I've thought about nothing but this moment for the last week, I've barely slept, and when I have I've dreamt about this moment, and the best I can come up with is 'Where did I get my shortness from?' Talk about banal – I mean it's hardly life-affirming stuff.

'Your father is tall, so are some of your brothers, and your sister, but your mother, she was small, petite – just like you.'

My father is tall. Is tall. Not was tall, but is. And so is my sister. I have a sister. Not a half-sister, but an actual blood sister. Older. Taller. And what does he mean by 'some of my brothers'? Some. What does some mean? More than one, I know, but 'some' makes it sound like a posse of them, like more than two for a start. If it's just two he'd say 'and so are your brothers', but 'some of your brothers', how many is that? Hang on. Even my older sister is taller than me. Typical.

'So my father is still alive?'

'Of course, yes. He's an old man now, but he's still alive.'

I can feel myself welling up. He's still alive. I haven't missed my chance; I haven't left it too late. If he's still alive now, while I'm sitting here talking to my cousin, then there's every chance I could meet him, face to face.

It's at times like these it'd be handy to have a religion. If I believed in a god, I'd have someone to thank, and it'd be nice to have someone to thank. As it is I'll have to settle for my own version: my father is alive, thank fuck for that.

The drinks arrive, and this time the waitress seems to dawdle for an age. How long can it take to put down a coffee and a beer? Can't she see we want to be left alone? Finally she gives me a glass for my beer and turns on her heel.

'What was my mother's name?' I blurt out.

'Hidat.'

'How old was she when she died?'

'Twenty-five or twenty-six,' he says.

Twenty-five? I'd assumed she was relatively young, but it had never occurred to me that she'd only be in her twenties. Twenty-five, that's nearly five years younger than I am now. My mother was younger when she died giving birth to me than I am, sitting here, hearing her name for the first time. I have already lived five years more than my mother did – that's a fifth more. I have lived a fifth longer than she did, and every day I live between now and when I die, that will be another day more than she did. Every day I waste, every afternoon I lose in a pub, every morning I languish in bed, are days she never had. Going by what he said before, by twenty-five, when she died, she had already had at least five children. And here I am, five years older, having done what exactly with my life? Bought shoes. Written about make-up, damaged my liver. I can't even remember what I did to celebrate my twenty-fifth birthday. It would have been 1999, so I was still with my last serious boyfriend, living in a dream flat in the Barbican. I was probably already getting excited about the snowboarding trip to St Moritz we planned to take with friends to celebrate the millennium. I wonder if I'd have enjoyed it so much had I known then that I was already older than my mother ever was.

I zone back in and realize Gaim is still talking, saying something about half-brothers and -sisters. 'After your father remarried' is all I catch.

He remarried? Another thing that hadn't even occurred to me. In the ten years since I'd known my father was alive, I had never once pictured him with anyone else. It had always been just him, on his own, missing his wife, struggling to bring up his sons. I'd often wondered if single-parent households headed by a black father were as rare in Eritrea as they were in England. I'd felt guilty not just for taking my brothers' mother away, but for making my father a widower from the moment I was born. But if he remarried, then that's not quite so bad, is it? I mean, my arrival still pretty much wrecked the family, but if he remarried, and had more children, then he must have gotten over it a bit, moved on at last, found closure, as Oprah would say.

We stay and chat some more. Gaim tells me about the rest of his family. My family. Every time he includes me in the equation, says 'our grandparents' or 'our aunt', for example, it's a surprise. These are not words I am used to. No one has ever spoken to me like that. Sure I've had grandparents of sorts – like my dad's parents. His mother, especially, I used to think of as my grandmother. She'd look after me in the school holidays, play with me in their garden in Little Sutton, near Liverpool. Let me pick apples from their tree, smuggle me sweets when my dad wasn't looking. I was about nine when she died from lung cancer, and that was the first time I remember seeing my dad cry. I was sitting on his knee in the back room of our terraced house in south Manchester, and I didn't know what was more upsetting: the idea of never seeing Peggy again or the fact my dad was crying. She was one of the few people who made me feel totally accepted. Loved, wanted. But I'd never called her Gran, or Granny, or referred to her as my grandmother – it was always Peggy. Just like when my father married his second wife, Claire – to me her parents were Brenda and Paul, even though to my brother and sister they instantly became Granny and Grandpa. It wasn't anyone's fault, it's just the way it was.

Gaim tells me about his brothers ('your other cousins'), many of whom are living in Sweden, having left Eritrea because of the war. He tells me how, because they were the branch of family nearest, everyone back home had expected them to find me. Before he left Eritrea, his brother Kelata tracked me down to Sudan. But when he went back, I'd gone. Then he tracked me down to Norway, and when they moved to Sweden they went to visit the Norwegian family who were looking after me, but I'd already left for Manchester. The Norwegians wouldn't tell him where I was, so he lost me again.

'It was awful for my brother,' says Gaim. 'He kept finding

you, telling your father, then losing you again. After you left Norway the trail went completely cold. Until your dad left that photograph in the orphanage. Then, at least, we knew for sure you were in England. When I came to London the pressure from the family back home got worse. They thought I wasn't trying hard enough. How could I be in the same country and not find you? I couldn't believe it when you got in touch and told me you worked at the *Guardian*. I've read your articles, I've seen your picture in the magazine, you've been right under my nose, in my house even, all along.'

'Will people be pleased to see me or will they be angry that I left it so long?' I ask.

Gaim looks shocked. 'It will be the happiest day of your father's life.'

I want to ask why I was put in the orphanage, but the question doesn't seem right. It feels too much like I'm accusing him of something. Also, I'm not sure I'm ready for the answer, so we talk around the subject some more, but by now I'm having problems concentrating.

Two things are swimming around my head. My father is still alive, and I look like my mother. I can't take in any more information. I just want to be on my own with these two new facts of my life. I'm Hannah. My father is still alive and I look like my mother.

I excuse myself and go to the bathroom. I lock the door, turn on the taps and splash my face with water. I look up into the mirror and mouth the words, 'My father is still alive and I look like my mother.' I say it again and again, several times over, like it's a confession, just trying to get used to saying the words, to rolling them around in my mouth as much as hearing them. I picture being in a bar or at a party: someone asks me who I look like – 'I look like my mother,' I tell them and when they ask where she lives or how old she is, I will say, 'She died, but my father is still alive.' They wouldn't even know I was adopted from that. It sounds so simple, so normal. After a lifetime of having to excuse myself, of dodging the simplest of personal questions – questions such as 'Who do you look like?' – because I didn't know the answers, I can now look people in the eye and give them a proper answer. It's like a huge 29-year-old weight, the weight of always having to explain myself, of dreading the next seemingly innocent question, has been lifted from my shoulders. So is this what it feels like to be normal?

I leave the bathroom and make my way downstairs, back to my cousin (my cousin!). We chat some more and then it's time to leave. So we make an arrangement to meet again soon. I know I mean it and I'm pretty sure he does too, but right now I'm desperate to be on my own. I'm elated, on a high, I want to just run and run. I want someone to ask me who I look like, or if my father is alive. I want to telephone all the people who ever gave me that patronizing look when I told them I was adopted and didn't know anything about my family, call them up and put them straight. I want to track down the boy who bullied me in primary school, shouting 'Famine Victim!' at the top of his voice down the corridor whenever he saw me. I never had an answer because as far as I knew he was right. But now I know he's not. My father is alive and I look like my mother.

Gaim sees me to the platform, we hug and say our goodbyes, or rather, see you soons, and he turns to leave. He disappears down into the tube, and I'm grabbed by panic. I don't want him to go. What if something happens to him on the way home and this is the last time I see him? What if he doesn't want to see me again? By the time I get home he could have left an 'It's not you, it's me' message on my answerphone. Maybe I should run after him. Apologize for acting so oddly. For firing all those questions at him, like he had some sort of duty towards me, like he owed me an explanation. Tell him the moment went to my head, but I'm actually a pretty normal person. I'm just about to shout when my train comes. I get on it, sit down, and burst into tears.

4

It takes me nearly an hour to get home, from west to east London, one end of the grotty District Line to the other. I turn the key in my lock and remember how I felt when I left earlier today, marvel at how much I've learned in just a few hours and without doing any more than hop on the tube and go to the other side of London. God only knows what I'll be like going to Eritrea if this meeting had such a big effect. As I open my door, the land line rings.

It's Gaim, ringing to check I got back OK. It's good to hear his voice again so soon. He wouldn't be calling if he didn't want to see me again. For a first date, it didn't go so badly after all.

As soon as I put down the telephone a wave of exhaustion hits me. It's as if all the effort of the past week, all the expectation of the meeting, then the meeting itself, not to mention all that crying on the tube, have finally taken their toll. All I want to do is close my eyes and go to sleep. But I should call my dad. He knew I was meeting Gaim today and was probably worried. He's probably spent the whole day stressing about it, fighting the urge to call me.

It feels kind of strange knowing about my father, and my dad not knowing. Not quite like a betrayal, but like I'm protecting him from something. Like I'm protecting them both, from each other I suppose. And as long as neither knows about the other then they can both carry on being my dad and my father, both as important as each other, no questions asked. No weirdness, no worry about being usurped, replaced or not worthy of the title. At this very minute I have two fathers but because no one else knows, it's simple. Perfect even. Not a bad compensation for not having a mother. As soon as I start to talk about it, I'll have to analyse it, make some sort of a choice. Even how I refer to them takes on a huge meaning, new meaning. Which one is the real one? In my head I have already separated them. One is my dad, and one is my father. One brought me up, wiped my snot, kissed my scraped knee. The other I came from. One I am for ever tied to by a shared history, the other by shared genes. One couldn't look less like me, the other I have nothing in common with. One understands me, the other looks like me but we don't even speak the same language. Nature verses nurture doesn't even come close.

But right now, here, alone in my flat, in my head, they can coexist. It doesn't matter that there are two of them. It doesn't need to be any more complicated than that. Any deeper. The reality of them both isn't a problem, it's a blessing.

I'm still toying with whether or not to call my dad. What if I sound too pleased when I tell him that my father is still alive? He might think I'm saying, 'Thanks for looking after me for the past thirty years, but it turns out my birth father is still alive, so I don't need you any more.' How will my sister Lydia feel if I tell her I've got a sister, older and taller than me? Will Tom think he's been usurped by not one, but three (as it turns out) older brothers? I could try to hide the excitement in my voice, but then isn't that a betrayal of my family in Eritrea? Isn't that like saying they don't really matter? I fall asleep on the sofa trying to figure out what to do. When I wake it's gone midnight. Too late to call, I decide. I climb into bed, relieved at having the decision taken out of my hands. I'll call first thing.

Except I don't. I wake up, feel a rush of adrenalin as I remember how well the meeting with Gaim went, followed by a big old truck-load of guilt as soon as I remember falling asleep on the sofa without calling my dad. I'll call later, from the office. That way I can cut things short, blaming 'work', if the conversation gets a bit tricky. By the end of the day, I still haven't called. There just didn't seem to be a good time. An open-plan office is hardly the perfect setting for such a personal conversation. Whenever I gear myself up for calling, there are either too many people around my desk (too public) or not enough (too quiet so everyone will hear). Besides, it was a really busy day. I'll call from home this evening. After a quick drink with the girls.

I didn't mean to stay in the pub so long. Now even if it weren't too late to call, I've had too much to drink, and even I know it's probably not a good idea to call him when I've been drinking. I want to be in control of the conversation, not struggling to remember what I've just said. The next day, the fact I still haven't called follows me around all day like a guilty smell. It wasn't tiredness that stopped me calling on Sunday, it was selfishness. I didn't call because I couldn't face it, because I wanted to keep my father to myself, mine alone, uncomplicated, for as long as possible. Worse than that, I wanted to keep my father a secret from my dad. And now my dad is definitely going to think something is wrong, or things have changed. How can I expect him to believe everything will stay the same after I meet my father in Eritrea if I don't even bother to call him after I've met my cousin in west

London? Why didn't I just call straight away, or at least the next day? Idiot. Talk about falling at the first hurdle.

Once in the office, I lose and gain my bottle at varying intervals. At least twice I dial the familiar number of my dad's house and both times hang up before it even goes through. I'd make a rubbish stalker. On reflection (i.e. bottle being lost once again), I shouldn't really be making a personal call at work: I'll call tonight on my own bill. Best to do it in a comfortable environment.

I get home, take off my coat, find the packet of cigarettes I bought before I met Gaim, dig out an ashtray, wonder why I gave so many ashtrays away when I gave up smoking, pour a large glass of red wine, take a gulp, and call my dad. No answer. The damn thing goes straight to answerphone. Might as well leave a message. I wonder if I should go for something succinct and to the point like, 'Hi, it's Hannah, my father is still alive and I look like my mother,' which, though a tad blunt, does get the message across, and is nicely unemotive, which has a definite plus side. But I opt for my usual approach, when I'm nervous: witter on for a few minutes, trying to sound as chirpy as possible. The usual banalities pour out of my mouth – 'Hope all is well, work's great, just ringing for a chat really, how are the kids, hi Tom, hi Lydia,' and I hope he can tell by my tone that what I really mean is, 'I love you, sorry for not calling sooner, sorry for putting you through this.' Midway through my by now rambling message, my dad picks up the telephone. 'Hi, I'm here, I was just in the kitchen cooking. How did it go? Hang on, before you start let me just get a glass of wine, and an ashtray.'

5

The next few weeks pass in a daze of planning and phone calls. I speak to an array of cousins from all over Europe. I learn of nephews and nieces in America. Of others in Saudi Arabia. My telephone rings pretty much off the hook and I come home most evenings to messages from new relatives. I get different nuggets of information with every call. I'm starting to piece together the genealogy, though it's not easy. Every time I ask someone how I'm related to them, they all seem to reply: 'I am your cousin.' After a few calls I am getting completely confused. Occasionally I ask if they are my father's sister's son or my father's brother's son. At which point they laugh and say no, describe some altogether different blood link, and when I express confusion, tell me not to worry about it – 'All you need to know is that I'm your cousin'.

It is hard not to get annoyed. When you've spent all your adult life wondering about having any family at all, it's more than a little frustrating for everyone to describe themselves in the same manner. I have had enough of grey areas: I want facts, specifics – times, dates, mothers' maiden names.

Eventually, I realize no one is being deliberately vague: cousin is simply a shorthand. It means you are related, but not necessarily as closely as cousins. If someone is related to you, but not your immediate family (i.e. partner or sibling) then the chances are they are your 'cousin'. And when I think about it, it's so much warmer than saying 'first cousin twice removed'.

A few weeks later I learn that Manna (Gaim's brother and my father's sister's son, since you ask) is going to Eritrea in June. I had planned to go in May, but after speaking to him I decide to put my trip back, so it can coincide with his. His daughter is sixteen and it will also be her first visit. This cheers me up enormously, until I learn she speaks Tigrinya. So I add feeling inadequate next to a sixteen-year-old to my ever increasing list of fears about the trip.

As well as dealing with the almost daily phone calls from new-found relatives across the world, for many of whom English is a third or fourth language, my time is suddenly taken up with organizing the trip, anticipating the trip, and trying to convince myself I haven't made a huge mistake. I see good and bad omens everywhere, and anything to do with the trip takes on great significance. It takes me a couple of weeks to pluck up the courage to go to the embassy for my visa. What if I'm refused a visa for some reason (because they can tell by the guilt in my eyes how long I took to reply to the letter)? What if there is some sort of authenticity test before you are allowed in? I'd fail that for sure. In the end, the only thing that makes me go is no longer being able to deal with the worry that I might be refused a visa. It turns out that the Eritrean Embassy is in Angel, Islington, no more than a ten-minute walk from where I have worked for the last seven years. I must have walked past it many times, and if I'd bothered to look up I might have noticed the flag, but then again there's no guarantee I'd have recognized it.

The sign on the door says the embassy will be open in five minutes. As I wait, an Eritrean woman joins me and we form the beginnings of a queue. It starts to rain. The woman says something to me in Tigrinya. I take a chance and ask, in English, if she wants to share my umbrella. She smiles, replies that yes, she would like to, in English, and we stand for the rest of the time in silence. I feel like I've failed some sort of initiation test by resorting to English. After I've worked myself into a state for a few more minutes, a woman opens the door and says something to us both in Tigrinya. The other woman replies. The embassy woman turns to me, repeats her statement (or was it a question?) and looks at me expectantly. I mumble that I don't speak Tigrinya, in what I hope is a suitably apologetic voice. The woman smiles, nods and looks at me sympathetically, and says, in English, that they'll be open in five more minutes. Before she shuts the door in my face, she says something to the other woman. They both laugh. I wonder what the word for 'paranoia' is in Tigrinya?

Once I'm inside the embassy things get progressively worse. I loiter in the lobby for a while, hoping someone or something will tell me where to go. A sign will do nicely. At least I wouldn't have to interact with a sign. Nothing is forthcoming, and I'm starting to feel like a complete simpleton, and an obvious one at that. I opt for the first office to the right. A thin middle-aged man comes out and starts speaking to me in Tigrinya. Needless to say, I haven't got a clue what he's on about. Nevertheless, I try to look as if I understand, though I don't know why I bother as I'll be breaking my own cover in a matter of seconds. When I think he's finished, I smile my apologetic smile, and reply in English that I'm here for a visa. I figure that if I just ignore the fact that people keep speaking to me in Tigrinya they'll eventually stop it.

It doesn't work. The man replies in Tigrinya.

'I'm going in June?' I say, hopefully.

He says something else, and walks away.

I look around, see a sofa behind me and assume he told me to sit down and wait, so that's what I do.

A couple of seconds later he comes back looking confused. 'What are you doing? Why haven't you come through?' he says in English.

'I thought you told me to sit down,' I reply, hopefully.

'No, I told you to follow me.'

So much for my language skills. If this is what it's like in the embassy, where I am effectively on home turf, what on earth is it going to be like thousands of miles away? I make my way to the office, feeling like I've been caught cheating in a test.

'What is the purpose of your trip to Eritrea?' asks the man sternly.

I tell him the shorthand: 'I was born there, but I left when I was a baby. I have family there I have never met, and that's the reason for my trip.'

He looks at my passport. 'Pool. That is not an Eritrean name,' he says, somewhat accusingly.

'No, but look,' I say, 'my middle name is Azieb, that's Eritrean, and look, it says there that I was born in Keren,' hoping those two things somehow right the balance.

'Explain Pool,' he says.

'I was adopted,' I reply.

Silence.

'By an English couple,' I add.

More silence.

'Actually she was American, but she died when I was young, in Sudan, that's where we lived. But they were white, well, they still are obviously – well, he is, she's dead, like I said.' I'm waffling now but I can't seem to stop. 'That's where Pool comes from. It's my dad's family name. But they kept my Eritrean name so I would always have a connection. And my dad always told me lots about Eritrea, it was just that I didn't want to know. But now I do. I want to know everything. That's why I want to go. In June. That's what I need the visa for. Please.'

The man seems surprised that I have come to a stop. 'What does your dad think of your trip?' he says, his tone considerably softer.

'He's fine with it; he offered to go with me but I think I need to do this trip alone.'

'He sounds like a very caring man. Fill out this form.' He hands me a form. My heart sinks when I see it is written in Tigrinya, but I recover quickly when I see underneath the Tigrinya is English. I look at the Tigrinya, its Arabic-looking script, and I feel totally overwhelmed by it. I won't even be able to read road signs. The sheer magnitude of what I'm doing hits me. I haven't got a bloody clue. It's hard enough trying to get the gist of what people are saying from their tone of voice, but on paper I haven't got a hope of understanding it. It's not like a European language where I can at least have a go at the words phonetically – it all looks so bloody foreign.

Deflated, I struggle through the form and hand it back to the man. He tells me to come back the next day, which I do. I flick excitedly through my passport and get to the page. I scan the green piece of card that is the visa. Under 'reason for visit' it says 'family visit'.

'You must come back and tell us how it goes,' says the woman who'd opened the door earlier, as I leave.

★

Now I've got my visa, I can book my flight. I can't go direct from London. The best options seem to be via Rome with Eritrean Airlines, or via Frankfurt with Lufthansa (due to Germany's kinder immigration policy there is a large Eritrean community there, hence the Lufthansa flight). The Lufthansa flight is the more expensive of the two, but something about Eritrean Airlines freaks me out. I don't feel ready for it yet. I keep imagining them, the crew and the passengers, all speaking Tigrinya and having a go at me for speaking English. I decide to give myself a break and book the Lufthansa flight.

I'm actually going. I have my visa, I have my tickets and I've had my jabs; the only thing left to do is sort out what the hell I'm going to wear.

Over the next few days I make a shopping list. At the top I write: 'Clothes – long skirts, long dresses, baggy T-shirts, trousers?' After speaking to my cousin I add the words, 'Not short, tight, no V-necks, no strappy tops, etc. etc. . . .'

Suddenly it's three days before I fly. Yesterday I had butter-flies for the first time. I was sitting on the Number 8 bus on the way home from work when I realized I was nervous. Not just job interview nervous, but nervous in the pit of my stomach – 'I can't eat or sleep' nervous.

Kelata, Gaim's brother and one of my new cousins in Sweden, rings me to tell me my three brothers, sister and father will be coming to Asmara to meet me. 'It will be the happiest day of your father's life,' says Kelata, which I know is supposed to make me feel better, but all it does is make me even more anxious. It's surreal enough as it is to talk about my father or siblings, without talking about how they'll feel when we meet. The whole thing has gone from an abstract idea, which I have been carrying around, brooding over for ten years, to a fixed event, with times, dates and places. I don't feel ready. This whole thing has gotten out of hand. It's gone from nought to sixty in under three months. Then again, will I ever feel ready?

The nearer it gets, the more resigned I become. I might as well do it now, go through with it now that it's all set up. It's only two weeks of my life, how bad can it be? I go, we meet, hate each other, I come back. What have I lost? It's not as if I ever really had them, is it? And at least when I come back I'll have an answer for all those people who bang on about how it's 'important' for me to go 'home'. I won't have to stand there listening to them patronize me about my 'lost identity'.

I wonder if they are nervous, my family? It's odd to think that they are getting ready to come and meet me, in the same way I am to meet them. Making travel arrangements, planning what they'll say. I wonder if my sister has bought a new dress, a short, low-cut one to make me feel at home?

Concentrating at work is impossible. Even when I do eventually manage to focus, it's only a matter of time before someone tells me how excited I must be. 'Try terrified,' I feel like answering, but don't. I get irritated with anyone who questions my faux chirpy 'I can't wait'. It's hard enough trying to believe my own bravado without having to convince others. I have a couple of low moments, when it all becomes too much. I dissolve in the ladies' toilets at work after a colleague tells me she'd be 'petrified' if she were in my position. In fact, I spend a good deal of my last week at work in the toilets, either quietly crying or just sitting trying to stem the panic.

The nearer it comes to my departure date, the more surreal it all seems, and the more I try to kid myself that it's not really that big a deal – all I have to do is get myself on the plane and whatever happens will happen. The wheels are in motion, and freaking myself out before I go away isn't going to make any difference to the outcome.

6

Finally, the day before I leave arrives. I have packed and repacked my bags several times over. I have to be at Heathrow at 7 a.m., but thankfully Linda, my dad's sister and one of my favourite people, lives in Teddington, not too far from the airport. Her husband, Duncan, has offered to take me to Heathrow, and Linda says she'll cook me anything I like the evening before I leave. Obviously I ask for the most English thing I can think of, a roast dinner. We eat, drink and chatter, hardly mentioning the trip, which is exactly how I want it. I go to bed early, saying goodnight and goodbye to Linda. We both agree it's probably a bad idea for her to come to the airport as we'll only start each other off crying.

I sleep remarkably well, considering. In fact it's the best night's sleep I've had for ages. I think it's because there is no more point worrying. I am going to Eritrea tomorrow.

Duncan wakes me with a cup of tea, I jump into the shower, get dressed, then kiss Linda gently on the cheek, making sure not to wake her as I know she'd see how scared I am and that would just make leaving harder. In the car, Duncan and I chat about everything and nothing. He tells me that if I need anything – money wired, an early ticket home, a friendly voice, all I have to do is call them and reverse the charges. I tell him to stop being so nice or I'll start to cry. After I've checked in, Duncan treats me to a farewell bacon sandwich. After we eat, we say a touching, but manly goodbye, i.e. no tears, for which I'm grateful. As Duncan turns away, I want to shout 'Don't leave me!' but I keep it in, and silently thank him for being such a man's man. If Linda had come we'd both be in bits by now.

As I go through to departures, I spot one of the men from my local Turkish kebab shop. I was in there on Tuesday and when I told him about my trip he gave me a great big slice of chocolate cake to celebrate my 'going home'. I wave to him and he sees me and waves back. In the departure lounge I stock up on newspapers and sweets – Werther's Originals because they are the most English thing on offer. I realize that without my mobile phone I won't have a clue what time it is, and that even if I knew how to ask a passer-by, I wouldn't be able to understand their response, so I treat myself to a bright pink children's watch, figuring it'll cheer me up if nothing else. I weave through the other travellers and make my way to my gate, only forty-five minutes early.

It's kind of a blessing to be going via Frankfurt. I can kid myself that I'm a normal person, just going to Frankfurt for work or pleasure. Just going to Frankfurt, that's all I'm doing, nothing weird about that. The flight is full of business people, no families and no large groups. It's pretty uneventful, but then that's exactly why I went for Lufthansa rather than Eritrean Airlines. I get off at Frankfurt with an hour to make my connection, so all I have to do is find gate A60 and wait to board.

And then I spot them: facing me, at the gate, are more Eritreans than I've ever seen in my life. The sight of them all freaks me out. I slow right down. There's no way I can go and just sit there with them all. What if someone starts to speak to me in Tigrinya? They'll know right away what a fraud I am. I decide to carry on walking, right past the gate, with an air of purpose, and take refuge in a cubicle in the toilets just beyond.

If seeing that many Eritreans in one place freaks me out, how on earth am I going to get on the plane, or get off it for that matter? I suppose I could spend the next two weeks in this cubicle. Or I could take a deep breath, open the door, apply some lip gloss and face them all. It's not even as if I know any of those people. What did I think people at a gate to board a plane to Asmara would look like? It's pretty obvious they were all going to be Eritrean. I'll just put my sunglasses on so no one will be able to make eye contact, go to the gate, find a chair and absorb myself in a book or something. Better still, I've got some nail varnish in my bag, so I'll paint my toenails. The toxic smell, combined with the look of concentration on my face, should keep away all nosey parkers. But first, a slick of lip gloss.

I find a seat near the window, so I can pretend to look at the planes in between coats of nail varnish. As I get the Dior baby pink out of my bag, I hear a bit of Tigrinya. I try to get my ears used to the sound as it floats above my head. It's not as if I haven't heard it before – ever since I moved to London I've grown used to Eritreans striking up conversations with me in the supermarket, in taxis, on buses. But it still sounds alien to me; the bits of German I can hear sound far more familiar. Tigrinya sounds like Arabic. Most of it seems to come from the roof of the mouth and the back of the throat. The written language is a form of script, with a different alphabet and different numerals, so I won't even be able to attempt to read or speak phonetically. And, according to my guidebook, even if there is the odd European word, on a menu for example, chances are, due to the legacy of colonialism, it will be in Italian, rather than English – so I'll be able to order pasta and say goodbye, but not much else.

I try to relax and look around, while avoiding eye contact. There are two or three men on their own, but mostly it's families or women travelling with children, and there are about fifty people in total. Most of the children are small, pre-school I'd guess, but I spot a couple of teenagers, studiously ignoring their parents, sitting with Walkmans clamped to their ears or playing on hand-held computers. Quite a few of them seem to be wearing braces. Hang on, braces? Isn't that the prime signifier of an American teen? I remember actually wanting braces after reading about them in a Judy Blume book. At one point I got it into my head that my lack of metal mouthware was proof that my dad didn't love me enough, and that he'd have cared more about my teeth if I was biologically his. 'If you loved me you'd let me have braces,' must have been a pretty tough argument to reason with.

'Are you Eritrean?' asks an American voice. It's a girl, about fourteen years old, with braces and a Reebok tracksuit.

'Yes,' I reply, intrigued by her Deep South accent as much as by the fact that she looks so American.

'Oh,' she says, not bothering to hide her confusion.

'Are you?' I ask.

'Of course I am,' she replies, climbing several octaves higher. She stands there for a second, then she mumbles something into her Reeboks and scuttles off. I go back to my nail varnish, wondering what that was all about. A few minutes later, she's back, with what look like her younger brother and sister.

'Excuse me,' she drawls, Britney Spears like, 'you're Eritrean, aren't you?'

'Yes, I just told you I was – why else would I be waiting for this plane?' I try to sound friendly, but it comes out all Mary Poppins, the way I always speak when I'm talking to Americans, especially those who practically faint at the sight of a black person with an English, or as they see it, white accent.

All three of the little Americans look at me like I've grown another head, a mix of awe and disbelief. I feel like telling them they're the ones with the weird accents, but they are children, so I merely scowl, hoping they'll leave me alone.

'You don't look Eritrean,' whines the boy, who looks about twelve, give or take the braces, which definitely take years off a man.

I'm stumped. I have never, ever been told I don't look Eritrean. Other Eritreans can spot me at twenty paces. There are many things in my identity I am not sure of, but whether or not I look Eritrean has never been one of them. Despite this, all I can muster is a rather lame, 'Yes I do.'

'No. You look like one of those London folks,' says the boy, as if to put me in my place. I burst out laughing. 'I am. I live in London. I grew up in England.'

The awe and disbelief are back. 'Wow, you have the accent and everything,' says the boy, pleased with himself. A couple of seconds of silence, and then he shouts, 'Mom, she is Eritrean, she's one of those London ones, with the accent and everything.'

So now the whole gate knows. Everyone openly looks me up and down, and those with travelling companions bow their heads together and pass verdict on this latest bit of information. Some nod and smile at me while doing so, but most don't bother. So much for not drawing attention to myself. Before the trio run off, I ask the girl where they are from. 'Dallas,' she giggles. Well, that explains the drawl. Now that my cover has been broken, I may as well have a good look at the other travellers. After all, they've had a good look at me. There's actually quite a large American contingent, including a man on his own, in his early forties, dark but definitely Eritrean, wearing chinos and a white shirt with an American flag on the front emblazoned with the words 'Let Freedom Reign'. Directly in front of me there are two girls, five or six years old, who have obviously just met. The older-looking of the two is singing her name like she's practising to be a cheerleader:

'Give me a G. Give me an I. Give me an N. Give me an A. What have you got?'

'Gina!' yelps the other, with delight.

'Now you do yours,' says the older girl.

'Give me an H. Give me an A. Give me an N . . .'

It can't be, I think. If her name is Hannah then that's got to be a good omen. She carries on: 'Give me another N. Give me an A. Give me an H. What have you got?'

I just about manage to resist the urge to scream, 'Hannah, that's what you've got!'

The girl shouts her name, and mine, and they jump up and down, holding hands and repeating, 'Hannah, Hannah, Hannah!' Well, at least I won't be the only Hannah out there.

At last we are told to board the plane. I walk up the steps and am greeted by the air stewards. I walk along the plane, and it occurs to me that not only is it full of black people, being served by white people, but it's a planeload of Eritreans, and I'm one of them. It's the exact opposite of my usual flying experience where it's always a pleasant surprise if there's another black person on the plane, and I'll smile and nod at

45

them like a friend, knowing they are as pleased as I am not to be the only black person on the plane.

I find my seat and sit down. I've done it. I've got myself on a plane bound for Eritrea. For the last few weeks, ever since I got my visa and bought my ticket, whenever I've had a bit of an emotional wobble, I've just pictured myself on the plane, ready to take off. This has been my goal, because I knew that if I could just get to this moment, everything else would take care of itself. To keep my side of the bargain, all I have to do is get myself on the damn plane. All I have to do now is go with the flow. And then it dawns on me. Over the next few weeks, whenever I have a wobble, all I have to do is picture myself on the plane on the way home. That is my new goal: to get myself on the plane home.

There's some sort of commotion in the seat across from mine. From what I can make out an Eritrean woman in her early to mid thirties and her two small children have been given seats on different rows. I automatically try to offer to move seats, but that won't help much. She's speaking to me in Tigrinya, but it's obvious what the problem is. What she needs is for the two men in the next row, the only white passengers, to move across.

After avoiding everyone's stare and muttering not very quietly to themselves in English for a while, clearly assuming none of us can understand them, one of them turns around and shouts, 'I HAVE TICKET, THIS IS MY SEAT, I AM NOT MOVING!' standing up and waving the ticket in the bemused woman's face for emphasis.

'She's not saying you've got her seat – she hasn't even asked you to move, though you could always offer. She's got two very small children and the airline has put them all on different rows.' I don't know who is more shocked by my outburst, me or him. He goes bright red, realizing I understood everything he said a few moments ago.

An air stewardess arrives on the scene. Says something in German. The man replies, sounding pretty fluent and very smug. The stewardess turns to the woman and speaks to her in German. I don't know what she's said, but her tone is patronizing rather than helpful.

The woman says something else in Tigrinya, shakes her head, points to her children, the tickets and then the three rows.

'I DO NOT UNDERSTAND,' bellows the stewardess.

'Is there a flight attendant who speaks Tigrinya?' I ask.

'No. German or English,' barks the stewardess, before turning back to the woman and repeating 'GERMAN OR ENGLISH?' at the top of her voice.

The woman, now on the verge of tears, starts speaking to me again in Tigrinya. An idiot could see why she's so distressed. 'She's not saying he's got her seat. She hasn't said a word to him. She's annoyed that despite the fact they could see at check-in that she is travelling with two small children, they've given her seats on different rows,' I hear myself say.

'Oh, right,' replies the stewardess. 'Thank goodness, someone who speaks English. Do you also speak German?' I shake my head. 'Well, you can help anyway, your English is very good, do you speak her language too?'

This woman needs a customer relations crash course, perhaps with a compulsory race awareness module, because right now she's acting like she's never seen a black person before, much less a whole planeful. I wonder if she's freaked out or annoyed at having to wait on so many of us.

'Can you ask her what the problem is?'

'I've just told you. She needs to be sitting with her children. If these two men would just move, then she could sit there.'

'We're not moving, these are our seats, we want to sit together,' says the man, sounding like a spoilt child.

The stewardess looks completely helpless and doesn't even try to reason with him. 'Can you tell her she'll just have to make do? The plane might empty out at Jeddah.'

'Jeddah is over five hours away, and besides, most people are obviously going to Eritrea.' I should probably add that I can't tell the woman anything as I don't 'speak her language' (despite my very good English) but for some reason I don't bother. I feel a solidarity with this woman. I feel like it's us, plus all the other Eritreans who are now giving us encouraging looks, against them. And I am enjoying it, though trying not to show it, obviously.

'Look,' I say to the stewardess, ignoring the two men. 'The seat next to me is free, but it's only a double and she needs a row of three. But if the men swap with me, then they can sit together, and I'll sit on the four with the woman and her children. I really don't know why those two are making such a fuss.' I point at each set of seats in turn, triumphantly. Hers, mine, theirs. One, two three, then shrug my shoulders. The quieter of the two men mumbles something to his friend. I wonder what they are doing, two German-speaking Englishmen on their way to Asmara. With attitudes like that they can't be diplomats or charity workers. Must be businessmen, come to bleed Africa dry, I decide.

The stewardess recovers her composure. 'Well?' she snaps, to the men.

'Well, I suppose we'd still be sitting together then,' says the loud one, only slightly sheepishly.

'Yes, of course, that's fine, we'll move right away,' says the other, with a sufficient amount of remorse in his voice.

'Ha! We win,' I think, but don't say. I suddenly remember the woman. I turn to her, aware and somewhat gutted that my knight in shining armour act is about to be shown up for the shallow thing it is – me trying to get on side with a planeload of Eritreans. But she says 'Thank you' several times, and passes me her toddler to hold while she goes to get her bags from the other seats. As we settle down for take-off, I do a quick count of the plane. It's pretty much full. I'd say two-thirds Eritrean, a third Arab in their white jellabas, and then the two white guys, one in regulation Gap chinos, the other in too-tight jeans, both wearing anonymous checked shirts and committing the fashion crime that is sandals with socks. Urgh.

I pop a Werther's in my mouth and offer one to the little girl sitting next to me. She looks about five or six, tops. She smiles for a second, then hides her face with her hand and throws herself into her mother's lap. Her mother says something to me, and I tell her I don't speak Tigrinya. She is surprised, but not judgemental. For the rest of the flight, we chat every so often in a combination of broken English and sign language. The toffees win over the little girl, and she goes from scared when I speak in English, to finding it hilarious.

There are an amazing number of languages on this plane. From my seat, I can hear English, German, Swedish, Arabic and of course Tigrinya. It's the most multicultural plane I have ever been on – it's like a flying Benetton advertisement.

I can't help noticing that everyone, myself included, looks

quite smart. It always amuses me that white people dress down for flying, thinking primarily of comfort, and black people dress up, thinking primarily of avoiding grief at immigration. I can guarantee that if I'm going through customs or immigration with a group of white friends I will be the only person stopped. The only time it didn't happen was when I went to Belfast a couple of years ago for a friend's wedding. I could barely contain myself when not one but two of the white friends I was with got stopped at Belfast Airport. I guess to the officials there I may have looked like many things, but IRA was not one of them.

I order a Bloody Mary to celebrate the fact I've made it on to the plane. I have a couple of glasses of red wine when they bring lunch around, mess about with my in-seat entertainment, get bored with watching Arabic television, read a bit of my book, and generally fidget for the entire flight. Thank God I'm sitting next to a child – I'd be driving an adult mad with all this twitching. What I really want to do is read my guidebook, but I feel like I can't. It would be an admission of failure somehow. It's bad enough showing yourself up to be a tourist when you're wandering around Paris, say, on a city break, let alone when you're going to the place you were born, to the place that is supposed to be 'home', your birthplace, your 'motherland'. If I sit here reading a guidebook everyone will know I'm not a proper Eritrean. Better to be a fidgeting, twitching freak than rumbled this early as a complete fraud.

After about five hours, we stop in Jeddah to refuel. All the alcohol is removed and all the Saudis get off. Apart from the two white men and the German crew, the plane is now an Eritrean-only zone. We may have come from all parts of the world but it's as if we are travelling as a large group, with the same purpose, except everyone but me knows what's waiting for them when we land. I was worried that I'd feel odd, easily singled out, on the plane, but now it's like I'm part of something much bigger than me, a pilgrimage of sorts. Our individual stories may be different, but the sum of the journey we are making is greater than our individual stories. The captain announces that we have one hour until we land. One hour? Is he mad? I'll never be ready to face Eritrea in an hour. Hopefully there'll be a spot of turbulence, or overcrowding in the skies, because frankly I could do with a couple more hours to prepare. I haven't set foot in this place for twenty-nine years, and now they're telling me I'll be there in an hour? There it is again, that dreadful sense that I should have been more careful what I wished for. One hour, that's nothing, it's less time than it takes me to get out of the house in the mornings. I've spent my whole life wondering what Eritrea is like – what it looks like, what it smells like, what it would feel like to step off a plane in Asmara Airport – and now, in less than an hour, I'll know.

7

'Madam, madam, you want some help?'

I've gone through immigration, such as it was, with a couple of men checking passports from behind a small glass box, and a middle-aged man in a well-worn blue boiler suit has spotted me struggling with my bags and is offering to help. Before I can thank him, he has loaded my bags on to a trolley and is pushing it at a rather alarming speed towards the exit gates. As soon as we get outside the main building, he stops, turns to me and gives me back the trolley. I thank him and make to turn away. He says something in Tigrinya. I shake my head, say I don't speak Tigrinya and thank him again. He holds out his hand. My heart sinks as I realize he's a porter and tips are how he earns his living. I panic and tell him I don't have any money yet, I've just got off the plane.

'A dollar?' he replies. 'You can give me a dollar.'

Relieved, I dive in my purse and pull out a pound coin. 'Here you go,' I say, proudly handing over the coin.

'What's this?' says the man, waving the pound in my face.

'It's a pound coin,' I reply.

'This is not a dollar.'

'No, it's a pound. I've come from England, not America, this is all I have. Pounds. Sterling,' I say, acutely aware of how plummy I sound.

The man is looking at the coin with disgust. 'What can I do with this rubbish?' He's shouting now, and others are looking, making me feel like some cheap tourist trying to get out of tipping the locals. 'It's a pound, a pound is worth more than a dollar,' I plead, to everyone around as much as to the man himself. The man shoves the pound back into my hand and spits on the floor. I scuttle off, shamed, get into a waiting taxi and give the driver my hotel address. It's not quite the homecoming I'd had in mind.

As the taxi moves I peer silently out of the window. It's pitch black, so I can't see much. I can make out a handful of buildings, but most of the light comes from the headlights of passing cars, of which there are few. It's frustrating to have arrived so late, when it's so dark, but it's also a blessing. I can slip quietly in by cover of night, no fuss, no fanfare, just check myself into my hotel without anyone noticing. And then, in the morning, I'll be here already, part of the furniture, nothing special, no big deal.

I barely notice the hotel decor when I check in, but I'm pleased my cousin arranged it all as it seems fine and, more importantly, they don't seem remotely fazed by my complete lack of Tigrinya. Once in my room, I can't decide whether to unpack now, so I'll feel a bit settled when I wake up, or to go straight to bed and leave the unpacking for the morning. Maybe it'd be a nice displacement activity.

I opt for falling into bed and checking out the television, figuring unpacking is handy to have on standby in case I can't sleep. I really hope I can sleep. Then I remember I've brought some essential oils with me. Prevention is better than cure, I decide, so I douse my pillow in lavender oil, and get ready for bed.

Every few minutes, the thought 'I'm in Eritrea!' or some silly version of it – 'I'm brushing my teeth in Eritrea!' 'I'm going to bed in Eritrea!' 'I'm watching CNN in Eritrea!' – pops into my head. The combination of whatever mundane activity I'm doing, and the surreal reality that I'm doing it in Eritrea hits me every time. I can't stop being surprised that I'm actually here at last. My head is buzzing. At this rate I'll have to put the whole bottle of lavender oil on my pillow. I wonder if counting sheep will work in Eritrea – perhaps I should count goats?

The lavender oil must have done the trick, because I wake up to find the sun streaming through my window. I rush out on to the balcony and take a deep breath. My first morning in Eritrea. Although, judging from the brightness and the temperature, it could be early afternoon. I must be at the back of the hotel. There's a well-kept garden below, the kind that would have sun-loungers carefully arranged around it were this a Mediterranean hotel, but it doesn't look as if anyone ever hangs out there, apart from the gardener. There are certainly no sun-loungers, even though it's baking hot already, and there doesn't seem to be a bar, or a barbecue area or anything. Just beyond the hotel garden are what look like private villas, and beyond them a couple of official or corporate-looking buildings, slightly dilapidated (are those bullet holes I can see?), each no more than five storeys high. It's a peculiar combination, the cute, Mediterranean-looking villas with their lush borders, and then these run-down office blocks. I don't know what I expected, but it certainly wasn't lush or commercial. I can't help but feel a little let down, conned even, it looks so normal. I go back inside and take my watch off the bedside table. It says 7 a.m. I switch on the television – yep, 7 a.m., and it already feels warm enough to melt tarmac. Ah well, at least I didn't oversleep after all, but what am I going to do all day? I'm too excited to go back to sleep until a reasonable hour – perhaps I'll unpack and then go and look for breakfast. It'd be nice to walk around before the rush hour.

Unpacking takes twenty minutes, and after I've finished the room has pleasing touches of myself dotted around. Best of all is my make-up bag, bursting with the items that form part of my daily beauty regime, their familiar brand names standing out proudly in such foreign surroundings. I wish I'd brought a couple of photographs of friends and family, just to watch over me while I'm away. In the meantime, MAC and Lancôme will have to do as substitutes. I put my wash bag in the bathroom and empty out its contents: shower gel on the top left-hand side of the bath, shampoo on the right, just like at home, so I can reach for both with my eyes closed and know what I'm doing.

Having put on some lightweight combat trousers and a white T-shirt (the most innocuous outfit I can think of), I go downstairs, hand in my key, and then set off exploring. Directly outside the hotel there are more cute villas which could come straight out of *La dolce vita*. The streets are a labyrinth of potholes, and yet what pavements there are, are beautifully tiled. I'm just getting my head around the tiled pavement, when I turn right on to what, according to my guidebook, should be the main street in Asmara – Liberation Avenue. Stretching out in front of me is a wide palm-tree-lined road that looks more like a Riviera boulevard than any image of an African high street that you might see on the news. Liberation Avenue makes Oxford Street look like a slum. I stand there drinking it all in with a combination of awe and I'm not sure what else – pride perhaps? And then comes the anger: why did no one bother to tell me how beautiful Asmara was? All

I've ever heard about Eritrea is war, famine and drought. Is it really any wonder I've been scared of it for so long? And now I get here and it's all chic villas, beautifully tiled pavements and a palm-tree-lined boulevard for the main street. Sure it's shabby chic, but it's chic nonetheless, and it certainly isn't the diet of war-torn, famine-ravaged Africa I've been fed for the last thirty years. The street isn't just grander than I expected, it's busier. There seem to be two types of car, either a clapped-out Toyota or a pristine, white four-wheel drive bearing the letters UN. Many of the Toyotas are yellow, so I assume they are taxis, which adds yet another element to this confusing mix. Each car, no matter what type or condition, seems to be sounding its horn, and they are of course all driving on the right, which must be yet another Italian legacy. I walk the length of the street, enjoying the anonymity of the hustle and bustle. I could be a normal Eritrean, on her way to work.

Up close, the buildings look shabbier than their grand art deco fronts let on. Eritrea, and Asmara in particular, was supposed to be Italy's playground. Mussolini gave his architects free rein in the capital – hence the tiled pavements and the stunning villas. Even though time and the ravages of a thirty-year civil war have taken their toll, the place has aged incredibly well.

After about twenty minutes of strolling along one side of the street, I stop in a café at the bottom, just across from what, according to my map, is Victory Square. My cousin and my dad both warned me that the street names in Asmara have changed so many times that no one refers to them, but Eritreans must feel proud walking from Liberation Avenue to Victory Square.

I go into the café, wondering what I'm going to order, and

how I'm going to order it, when I spot bottles of Fanta lined up in the cooler, so I ask for one, and point to one of the pastries behind the glass. No point rushing things on the language front, after all. I gulp the sweet orange drink and wolf down the pastry, realizing the last thing I ate was a dry cheese roll on the plane, and pay with some of the nakfa I changed my pounds into before I left the hotel. I'm eager to get back outside. Sitting here I feel like I'm missing out on the world. I rush out and make my way back along the other side of the street.

Despite the heat, everyone is dressed very well. Most of the men are either in smart trousers and shirts, many with a jacket on top, or impeccable T-shirts with the usual Nike and Adidas logos. The women are either in long, traditional white dresses that look like they are made of natural cotton, or dressed in pretty much the same way as the men, or in modest but modern skirts and dresses that graze the floor. The attire of choice for teenagers seems to be jeans and a shirt, blouse or T-shirt, but nothing too tight. No one is in shorts, and there is not a bare torso nor a pierced belly button, which, I have to say, is something of a relief. Mind you, I haven't seen any builders yet, so who knows. There's another big difference which it takes me a while to pin down. It's not about what people are wearing or the language they are speaking, but it's no less obvious. It's the way everyone is walking, or rather carrying themselves.

At first I think it is the fact everyone seems to be strolling. It must be too hot to rush, I reckon. But it's more than that. It's even those not walking, just standing around, chatting in groups, waiting at bus stops. I even noticed it earlier when I was sitting in the café. Everyone looks so comfortable, so relaxed, walking around as if they own the place. So this is what black people look like when they are not having to constantly look over their shoulder, or justify their presence. When they are not always waiting for the next bit of aggro, expecting to be singled out, ignored or given too much attention depending on the situation. Right at that moment a white soldier wearing a blue UN beret strolls past, and yet another thing dawns on me. He is the first white person I've seen since I got here. I check my watch: I have been walking on the main street of a capital city and it's taken forty-five minutes for me to see a white person. I know exactly how he's feeling, and for once he probably has a sense of how black people at home, wherever his home is, feel.

By now I no longer care about looking like a tourist, so I stop outside the buildings and have a good look. I'm standing outside the wonderfully art deco building of the Cinema Romero, craning my neck to see the lettering, when a woman taps me on the shoulder and starts talking to me. She's pointing up and down the street. Have I been doing something I shouldn't have? is all I can think. Has she spotted I'm not one of them? The woman gets a piece of paper out of her pocket and waves it in front of me. Then it dawns on me: she's asking me for directions. Here I am, not knowing a soul, neck craning to see the top of every building, resigned to looking like the tourist I am yet trying so hard to blend in, and this woman has paid me the highest compliment of all – she thinks I look local. Poor thing, she's in for a shock. I smile as it hits me, and fail to stifle a little laugh. Then I shake my head and tell her that I can't speak Tigrinya. She looks confused. 'I can't speak Tigrinya,' I repeat, moving my hands from side to side for added emphasis and adding, 'English. *Inglese*,' and pointing to myself. Just as I wonder what I must look like, she bursts out laughing. Which I take to mean she understands. And as if to show me she does, she turns on her heels and walks away, laughing to herself and repeating *'Inglese!'* So much for looking like a local.

I reach a large grey building with the word Telecommunication on the front, in a bright blue neon which jars with the elegance of the rest of the street. I decide to go inside anyway and try and make some calls. My cousin gave me a couple of numbers, and so did my friend Winta (who holds the dubious title of being my one and only Eritrean friend; she grew up in Germany but my dad and her mother have been friends for as long as I can remember, as have we). I buy a phone card from behind the counter, with relative ease and a lot of pointing, and make my way to a booth at the side. I pick up the receiver and dial the first number – it's for Winta's aunt. I shyly try to ask, in my best guidebook Tigrinya, if Tiblez is in. After a couple of attempts, the phone goes dead. I hit re-dial and try again. The same thing happens. I give up and try another number Winta gave me, this time for her uncle. A child answers. I ask for Abraha. The child bursts out laughing. For a few minutes, I am on one end asking if Abraha is there, and she is on the other squealing 'Abraha!' and then laughing. My telephone credits are going down quickly, so I give up again, this time saying 'Bye'.

'Bye-bye,' says the little voice, over and over again, until I hang up.

I try the third and final number I have, one my cousin gave me. It rings and a young boy picks it up. 'Hello. Teame?' I say, trying hard not to sound as desperate as I feel.

The boy says something in Tigrinya and my heart sinks.

'Teame?' I try again, hopefully.

'He is not here, he will be back later, try at 1 p.m.,' says the boy, in near perfect English.

'Thank you, thank you so much. It's Hannah, Gaim's cousin – I will try later,' and then the money runs out. I don't know if it's relief at not having three disastrous phone calls in a row or if it's delayed jet lag, but suddenly I'm exhausted. I head back to the hotel for a nap.

The telephone wakes me up. 'Hello, Miss Pool, you have a gentleman calling for you.'

'Who?'

'Mr Teame.'

'Thank you, can you put him on?'

'Excuse me?'

'Thank you, you can put him on.'

'OK, I'll tell him you will be down in five minutes.' The receptionist hangs up before I can protest. He must be here – calling as in 'a gentleman caller' rather than as in calling on the telephone – so I get up, check I don't look too crumpled, and head downstairs. Sitting in the hotel lobby is a dark, very good-looking man, with an air of the elder statesman about him. He spots me and jumps up and offers me his hand. 'Hannah, I am so pleased to meet you,' he says, before giving me three bear hugs, swapping from my left to right side and slapping me heartily on the back each time. I feel a million times better – safe somehow. I didn't realize how alone I'd been feeling, how desperate I was to see a friendly face, to have someone to show me the ropes.

'Come, I'm taking you on a tour,' says Teame, to my delight. In the car he explains that he has retired and that he is one of my cousin Gaim's best friends from school. For the next couple of days, Teame acts as tour guide, lunch companion, chauffeur and social secretary – calling people on my behalf. He takes me to his home and introduces me to his wife and son. I thank the son for giving such a great telephone message, and we start to talk about football. Teame's wife cooks for me and playfully chastises him for letting me check into a hotel when they have a perfectly good spare room.

After lunch, Teame drives me around Asmara, pointing out the sights, filling me in on the city's history, pre- and post-colonial. 'The Italians thought of apartheid first. The city was divided into Italian areas and Eritrean areas. Eritreans were forbidden from walking along the Italian streets. Do you see the large cathederal? Well, that was for Italians only, the small church was for the Eritreans,' he says.

We come to a shanty town, which Teame describes as the ghetto area. There are entire families living in one room, with mud walls and a corrugated-iron roof and no running water. We head up the hill, past an army watch point, where the soldiers don't even have mud walls, just a tent to keep them out of the sun. We get out of the car at the top of a hill. There's a small building there, which Teame tells me used to be a restaurant and bar. The view is spectacular. I can see right across the city. The perfect guide, Teame points out different areas, mosques and churches, and he tells me which used to be the white-only districts, and which were the black districts. 'Everyone forgets how bad the Italians were: under them we had no rights, we had to beg for everything, in our own country, while they lived in villas and walked on tiled pavements.'

After driving around Asmara for the best part of the afternoon, I tentatively tell Teame how I think people walk taller here, or am I just falling into the Western anthropologist's trap of making stupid assumptions about 'proud Africans'?

To my relief, he smiles and then laughs and says, 'When you go from Africa to the US or Europe on a scholarship you get treated differently, badly, but it doesn't matter because you always have Africa, you can always come back. You will be different now you know you can always come here. If they treat you badly back at home, if someone is racist to you, it won't matter so much because now you know what it feels like to belong somewhere.'

Never mind 'citizenship' classes, a trip to their African country of origin should be on the national curriculum for every black child. No wonder black boys who have been written off by the English education system thrive the minute they go to the Caribbean. It's probably got nothing to do with the teaching methods – it certainly isn't about resources – but with this feeling that they belong.

'You think this is proud,' says Teame as he drops me back at the hotel. 'Wait until you see Liberation Avenue at 6 p.m. It's like the whole world is out there, proud.'

After one of our tours, I go back up to my room, lie down for a few minutes, wake up over an hour later and realize it's nearly six. With Teame's words in my head I freshen up and head back out. The pavement is packed. It's like a mini Carnival, only without the blaring sound system or the embarrassing police trying to dance. A float of dancers or dressed-up children wouldn't look out of place, though. Everyone is out, just sort of strolling around. The groups are young, old, single-sex and mixed. Everyone is holding hands, be they a group of teenage boys or an elderly couple. Everyone seems to know everyone else, and no one goes more than a few steps without stopping to loudly greet another – either with the three kisses or the shoulder greeting, where they touch right shoulder to shoulder, three times, while shaking hands.

Feeling conspicuously alone, I find a café and sit on one of the pavement seats. This time, I feel brave enough to order a tea ('*chai*'), but am completely flummoxed by the menu, so ask hopefully for another pastry. I need to learn some new words or I'll be on nothing but pastries for two weeks. There are several others in the café, sitting and watching the world go by, but mostly it's groups and I get the feeling those on their own are waiting for the rest of their group to show up, so they can then go and strut their stuff up and down the main street. I sit there for over an hour, and see some people twice, which means they must have walked the length of the street, then back again. A few people even nod and smile at me with recognition, which makes me feel less alone. Two beggars go past, which is a pretty low hit rate when you consider there is one at virtually every cash machine along Oxford Street. The presence of the UN, which this morning I found strangely glamorous, is now beginning to grate. I know they are here to help – either as peacekeepers at the border with Ethiopia, or in the form of its various agencies providing aid – but surely they could do so less flamboyantly? Even a relative outsider like myself can pick up the tension between them and the locals. And then there are local military police on pretty much every street, men and women completing their national service – considerably less weighty than their UN counterparts, but also dressed in army fatigues and carrying rifles. The one thing I don't think I'll ever get used to is the number of people with missing limbs, presumably as a result of injuries sustained on the front. There are wheelchairs everywhere, their occupiers just as likely to be young women as old men – a sad signifier of how many generations have been injured during the thirty-year war with Ethiopia.

As it starts to get dark, the street seems to be emptying and I wonder if I should head back to the hotel. The awful 'Viva Forever' song by the Spice Girls, released a couple of years ago just before they broke up, is playing on the radio. It's a little too surreal, even for me, so I get up and leave.

When I get back to the hotel Tsehainesh, a friend of Teame who we bumped into the day before, has left a message asking if I'd like to join her and her sister Nebiat for lunch tomorrow. I call back and say I'd love to. Tsehainesh and Nebiat grew up in London, having fled Eritrea when the Ethiopian military police came looking for their father, a minister in the suddenly deposed Eritrean government. They and their father escaped, but many of his colleagues and their families were executed, as was anyone else who stayed and openly opposed the new regime. After hiding out in a boarding school, Tsehainesh and her family escaped across the border into Sudan, and from there went to the UK. The girls' father died in exile, but they returned after the liberation of Eritrea with their mother, who was determined to end her days in her own country. It is now three years since their mother died, but both sisters have decided to stay on. When they arrived they spoke no Tigrinya, but now they are fluent, though not as fluent as their children, who know as soon as they set eyes on you whether to address you in Tigrinya, Italian or English.

I warmed to Tsehainesh as soon as I met her. She seemed so happy, so sure of who she was. She has spent most of her life as an Eritrean in London, and now, here she is, a Londoner in Eritrea. She is the first person I have met who has made me think it is possible to be both without going crazy.

Over a lunch of pasta with *berbere*, the hot Eritrean spice, the two sisters make me feel as if anything is possible. They warn me that my family will be shocked that I am not yet married ('At twenty-nine you will be considered too old even for the eighty-year-old man in their village,' laughs Tsehainesh). And they tell me not to take it too personally when people tell me I should speak Tigrinya, 'Just smile and tell them you are learning – that will keep them off your back,' says Nebiat.

Over coffee, Tsehainesh asks which orphanage I was in. I tell her I don't know, the only information I have is that the orphanage was in Asmara, run by Catholic nuns, and a Sister Gabriella oversaw my adoption.

'Sister Gabriella? She's at the Camboni mission – I know her really well, she's a wonderful woman. Would you like to meet her?' asks Tsehainesh excitedly.

I say yes without really thinking it through.

'OK, finish your coffee and we'll go,' says Tsehainesh.

8

Half an hour later, we are pulling up in front of the gates of the orphanage. A group of young men in military garb, each carrying a rifle, come to the gate. Tsehainesh speaks to them and they reply, shaking their heads. I sit there hoping we will not be allowed in. Tsehainesh has told me not to worry, that this is one of the better orphanages, but I can tell by how quiet she has become that she is worried we may have rushed into this. You can tell a lot about a country by how it treats its orphans. From the passenger seat I try to look beyond the wrought-iron gates. To my right is a basketball court full to bursting with children, mostly teenagers, with younger children crowded around the sides cheering, and directly ahead of me is a grey municipal-looking building.

Two of the young soldiers are now pushing open the heavy gates, and we are passing through them. 'What did you say to them?' I ask Tsehainesh.

'They said we couldn't come in without an appointment, but then I explained you were one of them, and they said then you are their sister, you are always welcome, but you cannot take any photographs.'

We drive along the path, past a well-kept garden and a play area. So far so good – we could be in a school or a hospital, and as yet nothing really screams 'Third World orphanage'. There is evidence of children – the basketball court, a couple of discarded tricycles and plastic toys lying in the dust – but few of them actually around. Just as I am wondering if I should have any feelings of recognition, Tsehainesh tells me there was a fire some years ago and a lot of the old buildings were gutted. We pull up alongside a row of squat buildings. 'We have to report to the main office and get a member of staff to show us around,' says Tsehainesh. We get out of the car and walk into a small office. A young woman in her early twenties starts to speak to Tsehainesh. From their conversation I pick up 'Sister Gabriella', 'London' and my own name.

'Welcome,' says the young woman, motioning for us to sit on the sofa behind us. As she walks towards us I notice she has a slight limp, the tell-tale sign of an injury sustained on the front. 'I am Aster, what is your name?' she asks.

'I'm Hannah,' I reply, taking a seat.

'I am afraid Sister Gabriella has gone to the villages, but I would be happy to show you around; it is always wonderful when brothers and sisters come back to see us,' says Aster in flawless English. 'What time were you here?'

'In 1974, from around May until October – I left when I was about six months old.'

'Then we really are sisters. I was also a baby here in seventy-four – we will have been in the same room. I have lived here all my life, apart from when I did my national service on the front, and now I help to run the place.'

The room is suddenly filled with emotion. We are all thinking the same thing: it could just as easily be me standing here with a limp from a bullet in my hip, and Aster standing in my place. I will the lump in my throat to go back down and the tears in my eyes not to fall. I look at Tsehainesh and see that even she has welled up. Aster takes an awkward step towards the sofa, and I stand up and meet her halfway. We

67

hug, and kiss several times on the cheek, and then break away with nervous laughter at the emotion of it all.

'Is Hannah your real name?' asks Aster, heading back towards her desk.

'No, when I came here I was called Azieb,' I reply.

'If you know your father's name I can have a look and see if we still have your files,' says Aster, excitedly.

'Asrat, my father's name is Asrat,' I reply, trying not to get too excited myself.

'Just give me a few minutes,' says Aster, diving into a huge filing cabinet to the left of her desk.

Tsehainesh and I sit back down on the sofa. She seems as nervous as I am. 'Eritreans are very good record-keepers,' she says, squeezing my hands tightly.

'Azieb Asrat!' says Aster, triumphantly, from the corner of the room.

'Yes?' I reply hopefully.

'Here is your file,' she says, blowing dust from a manila file full of papers. She hands me the file.

I read the words 'ERITREAN CHILDREN'S WELFARE SOCIETY: ORPHAN'S PERSONAL FILE' and immediately burst into tears. A few minutes later and I have composed myself enough to read on. The first anomaly is my name: in big bold letters it says, 'AZEB ASRAT'. I have always spelt it Azieb – that is how it appears on my adoption certificate, which until now was all I had to go by. I wonder when the extra 'I' slipped in? I carry on reading.

Grandfather's name: MEDHIN
Mother's name: HIDAT ZEROM
Parents: Alive – Dead – Lost: BOTH DEAD

District: KEREN
Division: ANSEBA
Village: BEKISHEMNOK
Sex: F
Religion: ORTHODOX
Age: 29 days
Admitted: 31–5–74
Discharge Date & Reason: 21–10–74 [no reason is given]

At the bottom of the page is a section headed 'Other remarks' under which is written a paragraph of Amharic, the official language of the time, which Aster says just confirms the information above.

Inside the file there are five sheets of paper, thin and fragile with age. The first page, headed 'Princess Tenge Work Haile Selassie Orphanage, Charity Organization, Asmara', is also in Amharic. 'It says here that you were born in Bekishemnok, that your mother died after one hour, and that you are an orphan. It has been signed by an official and witnessed by elders in Keren on the fifth of May 1966,' says Aster.

'May 1966?' I ask, confused.

'Yes, that is the Ge'ez calendar, the old Amharic calendar – it works out as 1974,' says Aster. She looks through the rest of the papers and tells me they all say pretty much the same, they are just signed by different officials. I turn back to the front of the file. My eyes are drawn to one line: 'Parents: Both dead.' That's where it all started, with that lie, and my life, my identity since that date, 31 May 1974, has been built on that lie.

My dad has always maintained that they were told I had no family, but I can't help feeling relieved to see it there on the file. In moments of doubt, I had told myself that I would understand if my dad had lied about me having no family to protect me, so I'd have no one to feel rejected by, and so I would never feel as if he had taken me from anyone. But now, here it is written on the file, parents both dead. He was telling the truth. And if he was telling the truth about that, well then he's probably been telling the truth about everything else.

I wonder how big a part the 'fact' I had no family played in why they chose me over, say, another baby in the room? I wonder what it said on Aster's file.

Who made the decision to kill off my father? Was it the orphanage or my family? Or perhaps it was those elders in Keren, thinking I'd have more chance of being adopted if I came with no strings, thinking they were doing me a favour. Wasn't it bad enough that my mother had just died? Did they ever stop to think what it would feel like to grow up thinking you have no family? To constantly have to describe yourself as an orphan and have a lifetime of pitying looks? Or to learn, after nearly thirty years, that your father has been alive all along? I have an overwhelming urge to cross out 'Both dead' and replace it with 'Father alive', but can see from the look on Tsehainesh's face that it's best to just go with the flow, so the lie stays, despite the fact I am meeting my father in a few days.

And then another anomaly of the file occurs to me. 'Age: 29 days; Admitted: 31–5–74.'

'They were only eight days out,' I say.

'Who were?' asks Tsehainesh.

'My dad has always told me that my birthday, May the tenth, was something of a guess, more of an estimate really. It's always been something that bothered me. If I was twenty-nine days old on May the thirty-first, then my birthday must be May the second.'

One of the main things I wanted to know when I started this journey was my actual birthday. When I learnt that Eritreans don't really celebrate birthdays I thought I'd never find out, and now here it is in front of me, on a scrap of paper that's as old as I am.

My birthday has always highlighted how different I am from everyone else. Every time it comes around or every time I fill '10 May' in on a form I am reminded of how little I know about myself. I feel fraudulent accepting gifts and guilty celebrating what I know is a lie. If someone asks me what time I was born, I fob them off. 'What time?' I want to scream. 'I don't even know what date!'

My birthday is also the one day when I can never escape from what happened when I was born: my mother died. So over the years my birthday has come to mean these two things: it's a made-up date, and it's the day my mother died, neither of which are much of a cause for celebration. I can never change the fact my mother died giving birth to me, but at least I now know what date that was, 2 May 1974. Damn, that means I'm older than I thought.

'Come, let me show you around,' says Aster, bringing me out of my thoughts. I feel as if I have been in the orphanage a lifetime, and I haven't even looked around yet. As we walk outside my fear of what the conditions will be like returns.

'We are more of a children's home than an orphanage now, as hardly anyone adopts,' says Aster. The orphanage has about three hundred children, from babies to the teenagers I saw on my way in. There are approximately eighty staff, many of whom have been here as long as some of the children. The corridors smell of bleach and powdered milk. The children, though all thin by Western standards, look as well fed and healthy as the others I have seen in Asmara, no more or less waif-like. Their physical needs are clearly looked after, but what about their other needs? This place is certainly better than begging on the streets, but it is no replacement for a family. The older children have a studied air of indifference to our presence, but the younger ones crowd around, slipping their hands into mine, and it breaks my heart that they might think I am a prospective parent.

'This is the baby room, it's for nought to six-month-olds. You would have been in this room,' says Aster, opening the door to a room filled with cots. From the moment I walk in I am struggling to hold back the tears. There are about ten cots in the room, each carrying one or two children. At one end of the room two women sit bottle-feeding more babies. As soon as I walk past the cots, those old enough crawl towards me and stretch out their arms, pleading to be picked up. Most do so silently.

'Don't be afraid, they just want to be held,' says Aster.

'Are we allowed?' I ask.

'Yes, of course, it is what they need,' she replies.

I turn to the nearest cot, and lift up a baby girl. It's that simple. She clings to me instantly. Is this how my parents chose me? After a while I put her down and pick up a boy. I am about to pick up another child when one of the women feeding says something and points to the cot I am in front of. 'Aster, what is she saying?' I ask.

'She says there is no point picking up that one, he is sick and won't notice.'

Entering the baby room was one of the hardest things I have ever done, and turning my back on it was even harder. That evening I go to bed feeling wretched, unable to shake the baby room from my conscience.

9

The next morning I wake exhausted. Teame and I picked up my cousin Manna, who'd flown in from Sweden, from the airport late last night. I was still in a bit of a state after the visit to the orphanage so I don't think I made a particularly good impression – still, hopefully he and his family were too tired from their flight to notice. When we said goodnight, Manna said he would call me today with the details of where and when I am to meet my family, which will probably be tomorrow or the next day. This means today is quite likely to be the last chance I have to relax, so I decide to take today 'off'. I go to the Mask Place, one of the few cafés with an English menu, and have hummus and pitta bread for breakfast. I go to an internet café and check my e-mail, something I have deliberately avoided until now as it somehow felt like cheating. Afterwards I sit outside a couple of cafés ordering Fanta and reading magazines I bought at Heathrow. For lunch I go to Casa Italia and have a glass of red wine with my pasta. After lunch, and feeling very much in holiday mode, I decide to do some surreptitious sunbathing on my balcony, while the rest of the city has a siesta. Having been warned how conservative Eritrea is I didn't even bring any vest tops, never mind anything resembling a bikini, so I strip down to my bra and the biggest knickers I can find, but only after checking I am hidden from all view. I want a tan, not to cause offence. I lie down on a towel, water by my side, headphones clamped to my ears, close my eyes, and try to imagine I am on a Greek island.

An hour and a half later the telephone wakes me up.

'Hannah, it's Manna.'

'Hi.'

'They're here.'

'Who's here?'

'Everyone – your family. I'm with them now – your father, your sister and your brothers, they're all in the same room.'

'But you said they wouldn't be here for a couple of days!' I say, hoping he can't hear the panic in my voice.

'Well, they're here now. I'm coming to pick you up, don't move.'

Move? I can barely draw breath. 'I need more time to prepare,' I plead, lamely.

'I'll be there in ten minutes,' Manna replies, before hanging up.

Ten minutes? Surely this is some kind of sick joke. All that waiting, all that expectation, and now someone is telling me I have ten minutes to prepare before I meet my family – and to think I panicked at only having an hour left on the plane. How can this be all it boils down to? My father, my sister and three brothers in ten minutes, that's precisely two minutes to think about each one of them, except it's probably a lot less now as I've been standing here for I don't know how long. Ten minutes is all that I can think of. If it takes Manna ten minutes to get here, it will take us ten minutes to get to the house they are in, so I suppose that's really twenty minutes before I come face to face with them, which is a bit better, but even still, it's not much after a lifetime of waiting. I knew at some point there would always have been a 'ten minutes' moment, but I thought it would be in a couple of days' time, and I'd be able to build up to it, have at least the day before, then a sleepless night before, then maybe a morning and then an hour, then half an hour and only then, after all that, a 'ten minutes'. That's how I'd imagined it. That's how it was supposed to happen. Not this – from a couple of days and then just leap-frogging the rest and going straight into the ten-minute count-down. You can't do anything meaningful in ten minutes – it takes me longer than ten minutes to plan what I'm wearing before I go to the office, never mind get prepared to meet my father for the first time.

What have I done? How did I get myself into this mess? How did I get to be standing here, in a foreign country, where I don't speak a word of the language (unless you count the ability to order tea), with ten minutes before a man I barely know meets me in the hotel lobby, and then takes me to meet a group of strangers, one of whom is my father?

Why did I start all this? I should have listened to all those voices – friends, family, and even my own – telling me to leave things as they were. 'Why open the can of worms?' they said. 'Isn't one loving family, no matter how unconventional, enough? That's more than some people have.' Why did I listen to the constant chatter of my own curiosity? I ignored all that 'who am I, where am I from?' stuff for so long – why couldn't I just have carried on as if it didn't really matter, as if I didn't really care? Ignoring it, instead of getting seduced by the promise of some instant, quick fix for all my problems. Short of jumping off the hotel balcony, there is no way I can get out of this now. This is going to be one of the defining moments of my life – I will never be the same again at the end of these ten minutes – and yet I am completely powerless as to the outcome. All I can do is go along for the ride.

I look at my watch and realize I've been staring into space for a full three minutes. I look down and realize I'm still in my knickers and bra, and remember the impromptu sunbathing session. I'm also sweating and streaky from the sun cream. I don't have much time left, so I jump in the shower, hoping I'll figure out what to wear while I'm in there. As soon as I'm in the shower, I start to cry. I seem to be doing a lot of that here, crying for no particular reason. Best not to wear mascara for the meeting, except now my eyes will be all puffy so maybe I'll wear a little bit, but just make sure it's waterproof. I fiddle with the temperature, figuring a cold shower might shake me out of this panic. It does the trick, my head clears, the tears stop and I start to feel more in control.

I get out of the shower and go back into my room. Damn, I was so busy crying like some kind of freak that I forgot to decide what the hell to wear. The telephone rings. I contemplate not answering it, in fact never answering it again. If I am quick enough I could throw some clothes on, leave the room, hide upstairs or something, wait for Manna to leave, sneak back when the coast is clear, pick up my bags and get the first plane out of here. I pick up the phone. It's Manna, he's in the lobby. I tell him I'll be a couple of minutes and as I put the receiver down my mind goes completely blank. Am I fainting? That would buy me some time. There was a girl at school who used to be able to make herself faint – why hadn't I paid more attention when she told us all once how she did it? I'm not fainting, I'm going to be sick. I go into the bathroom and retch a couple of times. Nothing but water and bile comes up, but I feel better, more focused somehow, like now I can concentrate on the matter at hand. Back in the bedroom I put on the dress I had planned to wear for the meeting, a calf-length loose-fitting number in natural linen. I wouldn't be seen dead wearing it at home, but it was the most demure dress I could find – everything else was either low-cut, not long enough, or more frequently both. It does, however, make me look like a sack of potatoes. It also feels completely wrong, it's just not me at all, as if I'm trying to be someone I'm not, which I suppose isn't far from the truth. This afternoon is going to be bad enough without feeling as if I'm in someone else's skin. Sod the dress, I decide, taking it off and trying on a white linen skirt and top combination that I also bought for the trip. As soon as I look in the mirror I realize it looks far too bridal. What was I thinking with all this bloody linen? Everything I've brought makes me feel like an extra from *A Passage to India*. I wish I'd brought something I wear all the time, something that would at least make me feel like me, instead of all these new clothes, designed not to offend but which make me feel like a fraud. Deciding to ignore the 'long dress or skirt is best' advice of the guidebooks, I settle on a pair of black three-quarter-length trousers and a loose, black top (in linen, of course), which make me feel much more like my usual self. I slip on my white Birkenstocks, look in the mirror, and am pleasantly surprised with the ensemble – it's the perfect lazy Sunday outfit. If only.

What I could do with now is a cigarette and a drink. But mostly, what I really want is more time – another twenty-nine years would do; or perhaps just a couple of hours, in a pub with a friend; or a hug from my dad. Instead all I've got is a few minutes on my own in this hotel room, just enough time to freak myself out some more. I don't even have time to call anyone. It feels like I'm about to jump out of a plane knowing there is no parachute, and that as soon as I leave I'll go into free fall.

I've thought about this scenario my entire life. Even when I thought I had no family, I still day-dreamed about a long-lost relative, my mother even, showing up and saying it had all been a big mistake. It's every child's fantasy, but for the adopted child it's more than that – it can give them hope that they were wanted all along. When I was bullied at primary school, and told to 'Go back to where you come from', I'd smile to myself and think, 'Just you wait, one day an African king is going to come and claim me as his long-lost daughter, and then you'll be sorry.' And yet now the fantasy is about to become true, give or take the regal element, I don't know if I can go through with it. If I just stay in this room for ever, my life will stay at this moment. Paused. The fantasy unblemished by reality. The picture I have of them in my mind, the picture they have of me, unspoilt. No question of them not liking me, no chance of me not meeting their expectations, which, let's face it, I'm going to be pretty hard-pushed to meet. I mean how can I be the perfect long-lost daughter, how can I be worth my father losing his wife, my brothers and sister their mother? How can they not resent me, wish I'd never been born, wish my mother had been the one to survive?

All the research into adoptees tracing their birth parents harps on about the fear of repeated rejection. That's rich. For a start it makes it sound like the rejection is all in the adoptee's head. Which it isn't, it's a fact. My family didn't keep me. It doesn't matter how honourable their motives were, the fact of the matter is they made a conscious decision to give me away, to stop caring for me. I had no say in the matter. I was a newborn baby. I was completely dependent on them, I needed them, and what did they do? They handed me over to strangers. So don't preach to me about my 'fear' of rejection, like it's some psychological flaw, unless you've been there, or unless you can guarantee me one hundred per cent that it will never, ever happen to me again.

I am certain a good deal of my personality is tied up with me being adopted. Everyone finds it hard to trust people, but adoptees find it nigh on impossible – and who can blame them when the very people they should be able to trust, their mother and father, turned their backs on them?

I've obsessed over what I would have been like if I had had a 'normal' upbringing – a 'normal Eritrean' one or a 'normal English' one. The location is almost irrelevant, to my mind. It's the normality, the not being given away, that would have made the most difference. And though of course there is no denying that, practically and materially, the outcome would have been very different, the thing that remains the same is the sense of belonging, that families are permanent. The almost invisible confidence that comes from knowing no matter what happens, your parents will always be your parents. No matter how often your adoptive family tells you they love you, no matter how much you believe them, for the adoptee there is always the knowledge that a parent can decide they don't want you any more, sign a few forms, and wash their hands of you. And if a parent can do it, then what's to stop others – friends, lovers, anyone? It's tattooed on your psyche: love is temporary.

So you toughen yourself up and tell yourself it doesn't matter. You swear to yourself (who else is there?) that you will never again end up powerless, you will never again be in a position where someone can let you down, give you up, reject you. You convince yourself you don't need other people. Sure, it's nice to have them around, but you don't *need* them. There is only one person in this world you can rely on, and that's yourself. In fact (you convince yourself), your birth parents probably did you a favour by making you realize this so early on. But having spent your whole life doing everything you can to make sure such massive devastation can never again be heaped on you, something starts to irk. It's not so much a flaw in your logic as a chink in your carefully constructed armour. No matter how convincingly you pretend otherwise, the desire to meet your birth family is always there, gnawing away at you. It's like an emotional pirate radio station: on some days the frequency is too weak to be picked up, on others it's impossible to ignore; it distorts every one of your thoughts.

But you're used to ignoring thoughts about your birth family, about what could have been. The real danger is if you do decide to listen to the voice, if you decide you can ignore it no longer. Because going in search of your birth family goes against everything you've taught yourself. It's setting yourself up for the mother of all falls, bad pun intended. The potential for rejection is only the half of it: it's the potential for rejection by the very people who gave you up – a double whammy. By searching out your birth family, you are giving them another chance to do the very same thing they did all those years ago, to wreck your life all over again. It's like the victim of a vicious attack asking their assailant if they would like another go.

I need a drink. I need a cigarette. I need someone to carry me out of this room. Oh man, what have I done? Why did I start all this? What on earth was I thinking? What did I think it would be like? It's only now that I realize I've never given any real thought to how I would feel immediately before meeting my family. It wasn't an oversight as such, more a coping strategy. Once I'd made the decision to come here, I knew that if I thought about things too deeply, for too long, I'd do my own head in, talk myself out of it. And as I had to come, as it had got to the stage where I knew there was no question of me not doing this thing, there seemed little point in freaking myself out. Oddly, I'd got beyond this point in my thoughts. I may not have thought carefully enough about the moments before the reunion, but over the years I've played out every possible permutation when it comes to how the meeting itself could go. Like I said, some ten-year-old girls plan their wedding day, but I planned the day I'd meet my birth family: what I'd wear, what the weather would be like, whether or not I'd have a friend with me. And for the last ten years, it hasn't been a complete fantasy. Ever since I got the letter from my brother I've known the question of a reunion was down to me, it was there if I wanted it, they were waiting – all I had to do was go to Eritrea. And ever since then, the scenes of me meeting whatever family I have left have been playing on a loop in my head. Other than myself, the main players are faceless, but it doesn't matter because I know they all look like me. I guess they're faceless because before I met my cousin I had no idea what a man who is related to me looked like, nor a woman. Sure I've seen Eritreans on the street who look a bit like me, but that's only in a relative sense, rather than a full on, bona fide, *related* one.

The opening scene is always the same. I am standing in front of a door. Someone else's arm (it's black, I think) reaches in front of the door and turns the round handle. Sometimes it's a round brass handle that turns clockwise, like the ones in my flat; other times it's a proper handle, I'm not sure what colour or material. Very occasionally, it's a Yale key. But it doesn't matter, because whichever it is, the person opening the door always seems to know. Once they turn the handle, they push the door open and as my eyes follow the sweep of their arm, it opens fully and there, as if in a line-up, are my family, faceless but there, like shadows. Sometimes the room is packed; at others, there is no one behind the door. It doesn't take Freud to figure out what's going on. On good days, everyone shakes hands (how English), kisses on the cheek three times Eritrean-style, and then sits down. The atmosphere is emotional, but not overwhelming – it's almost chaste. I instantly know who is who, and everyone, not least myself, is amazed by our physical likeness. We laugh the same raucous laughter, despite the fact we have never previously met.

On less good days, people start shouting at me pretty much as soon as I enter the room. They are speaking a mixture of English and Tigrinya, but I know they are all saying the same thing: 'Why didn't you write back?' 'Why didn't you come sooner?' and so on, while I just stand there, unable to answer their questions. And on really bad days? Well, on really bad days when the mystery hand opens the door, there are a group of people standing around an old man in a bed. The youngest of the group, a man in his early thirties, turns around and tells me that my father has just died.

If I stay in this hotel room for ever I will never learn which version, if any, is the right one, but right now that's preferable to taking the risk either way. As soon as I leave this room, a chain of events that are way beyond my control will start. My life will never be the same again: I will have met my birth family. In half an hour, I will have come full circle. The story of my life will be completely different. I will no longer have to dodge the simplest of questions, questions like 'What does your father look like?' or 'Who do you get your eyes from?' In half an hour I will know the answer. I will go from being the adopted girl who has never met her family, to the adopted girl who has. They are two very different people. How many changes of identity can one person take? I have already been an Eritrean daughter, Eritrean orphan, Eritrean adoptee, and now I am about to become an Eritrean daughter again. The nearer I come to meeting them, the nearer I am to becoming a completely different person, a full person, instead of one whose identity is dominated by that which is missing – my birth family. The way I think of myself in relation to the world, the way others see me, will change for good, and all it takes is for me to put one foot in front of the other, and leave this room. It's that simple. It's all I've ever wanted, and yet I am terrified.

Maybe if I focus on leaving the room, rather than on what happens afterwards, it will be easier. Set myself a smaller, more manageable target, to leave the room, rather than the Everest of targets, to go and meet my family.

'Count to three and just leave the room,' I say out loud. It's more of a dare to myself than a conscious decision. I leave the room and concentrate on trying to modify my breathing, hoping it will stop my hands getting clammy. Clammy hands are not what I want my family to remember about the first time they met me. I spot Manna sitting in reception, and go to join him. 'Do I look OK?' I ask, too nervous for pleasantries.

'You are fine,' he replies.

'Fine? Oh,' I say, dejected. 'Do you think I should change, put on a dress perhaps?'

'No, you don't need to change, you look fine. And anyway, we don't have any time.'

'Can't I have a drink first, a little something to steady my nerves?' I venture, realizing how bad this probably sounds to someone who's just met me. Still, he probably just thinks I'm a typical alcoholic Brit abroad.

'A drink? You want to drink now? Don't be ridiculous, now is not the time to be drinking. You can't smell of alcohol when you meet your father for the first time. There will be plenty of time for drinking later. Now we must go.'

I silently figure a cigarette is probably also out of the question. 'Should I take this off?' I ask, pointing to the silver necklace with the letter H on it that my friend Debra gave me for Christmas.

'Why would you take it off?' asks Manna.

'Well, I feel a bit awkward with the H,' I say, hoping I won't have to explain further.

'Why? It looks lovely,' says Manna.

'Yes, I know, but it's H for Hannah, isn't it? And that's not the name they gave me.'

'Keep it on, it's pretty. There is no need to take it off.'

'You don't think they'll be offended, or hurt by it? It's kind of blatant.'

'Not at all,' says Manna, but I am not convinced, and I want everything to be right, so once we get in the taxi, Manna in the front, me in the back, I quietly remove the chain.

As soon as the H comes off I feel naked without it. I thought taking it off would make me feel better; it had felt like a hot stone on my chest, or a flashing neon sign that read 'Not from around here'. It was the letter, rather than the necklace itself. It felt aggressive somehow, like I was using it to guard me against some sort of evil. And to remind everyone around me that my name is Hannah now, not Azieb, which of course it is, but there's no need to shout it from the rooftops. Then another thought enters my mind. What will they call me?

My dad kept Azieb as my middle name so I'd always have the option to use it if I wanted, but apart from a very short-lived Afro-centric period in my teens, during which I went out with a black guy called Sean who'd changed his name to Shakim, I have never contemplated changing my name. I was always thankful for the normality of Hannah. I didn't dislike Azieb, but I was always relieved it had been relegated to a middle name, and even then I would occasionally find myself embarrassed by it, by how foreign it sounded. At school or wherever, when people would start talking about middle names, I'd sit there willing the topic of conversation to change before it came round to me. Azieb just didn't fit with all those Ruths and Louises. As if it wasn't bad enough being met with bemused looks every single time I said it in a group, I'd then have to endure the usual rounds of 'Oooh, how exotic' and 'What does it mean?', followed swiftly by, 'So how come you've got that then?' And before you know it, I'm having to divulge the most intimate details of my personal life, and all because someone asked me my middle name.

No one has ever called me Azieb to my face. It has always been a name on a piece of paper, handy when I need an obscure password, but not something vocalized, not something I would turn around to. And yet here I am, in a taxi, on the way to meet a group of people who have never thought of me as anything else. Maybe they'll ask me which name I'd like to be called? The trouble is, I don't think I really know the answer. Hannah or Azieb? I'm both. Asking to be called Hannah, like wearing the letter H on the necklace, feels rude somehow, like I'm making some sort of statement, as if I don't think my Eritrean name, the name my father gave me, is good enough. But opting for Azieb over Hannah feels like a betrayal of my dad. Giving me the name Hannah was probably one of the first things he and his first wife, Marya, did when they adopted me: it's what made me theirs. It feels disloyal to cast it aside as if I've had a better offer. And yet, deep down, the idea of answering to Azieb really appeals to me. I want to know what it feels like to be called Azieb, to be an Azieb. To have my father call me by the first name I was ever given.

Maybe I'll be Azieb in Eritrea and Hannah in England. It's pleasingly simple and keeps everyone happy, including me. My dad won't know and my father won't be offended. I get to keep my identity as Hannah, but I also get to see what Azieb is really like. And thanks to geography, there is no reason why I can't keep them both going, running parallel to each other, at least for the time being, until the two are ready to meet.

I look out of the window at the twilit city and notice that we have turned off the main street and are now driving down what appears to be a dust road. Squat houses that look like they are made of clay have replaced the Italian villas. I try to look into the rooms, but it's hard to look past the beaded curtains that keep out the flies. I guess these are Eritrea's version of net curtains – not that unlike Manchester after all, then. The road is getting bumpier by the second, and just as I am about to express amazement that the car can manage, the taxi slows down to a halt. Manna jumps out and pays the driver. I look around and wonder which of the surrounding doors has my family behind it. It turns out none of them do. 'Follow me,' says Manna. 'It's just a short walk.' I can't help but be relieved we haven't arrived yet.

As he strides ahead I look at Manna and have an overwhelming wish that I was with my dad. If he were here now he'd know what to do. He'd know how to make this OK. He'd go into the room ahead of me, and only after having checked everyone out, and told them in no uncertain terms to be nice to me, would he let me come in. I chose to come here by myself, to go it alone, despite his repeated offers to come with me, because I thought it would be easier this way. I didn't want to have to deal with anybody's feelings other than my own. I thought if he came with me I'd spend all my time worrying about what he was going through, what I was putting him through, and I knew I didn't have the energy to look after both of us. But I see now that it would have been the other way around. He would have looked after me. He would have taken any flak on my behalf if I changed my mind at the last minute, gone into the room first if I'd asked him to, stayed at the hotel if that was what I wanted. And yet I said 'No thank you' to all of that. 'I'll be fine,' I'd said, and cruellest of all, 'I'd rather do this alone.'

I thought I was being strong by coming alone, and wise. If I can do this alone, then there's nothing I can't do, I'll be invincible. But now, coming here on my own suddenly seems foolhardy rather than brave. I have no idea what these people are like, I am in a foreign country, following a man I barely know into a house full of strangers. I'd never do that in England – what makes me think it's a good idea to do it now? Suddenly I am gripped by a *Daily Mail*-like panic. What if they are all part of some weird African cult? What if they try to marry me off? I won't even know what's going on because I never bothered to learn the language. It'll all be my own stupid fault for thinking I can just swan in like I'm some sort of visiting dignitary.

I don't think I can do this. I don't think I have it in me. Even if I manage not to offend them the moment I walk in, it is still more than likely that I'll fuck the proceedings up somehow. I am stunned by how unprepared I feel. How can you spend your whole life thinking about one moment – daydream it to within an inch of itself – and yet not feel ready when that moment comes? I can only assume that you are never ready.

As soon as I went public about my plan to trace my family, all sorts of people started coming to me for advice. People I had barely spoken to previously were suddenly telling me about the child they'd had adopted when they were eighteen, or how they'd found their birth certificate and discovered their father wasn't their 'real' father. It was like I became some kind of 'tracing' oracle. I didn't have the heart to tell them that I was winging it, that they might well be better off just leaving well alone, and so instead I'd offer vague platitudes, warn them not to expect it to be easy, and most of all, tell them to make sure they were ready. And now I know what I'd suspected all along, you can never be ready, not for something as big as this.

'It's this house.' Manna's voice brings me back to reality.

IO

We're here. We. Are. Here. I say the words over in my head, hoping the situation will seem real. I am standing on one side of a door, my father is on the other. It suddenly occurs to me that I no longer have any idea what I want the outcome of this to be. I got so caught up in just getting myself to this point that somewhere along the line I forgot why I was doing this. And now I barely know what I want to happen when I walk into that room, or even what I want to see when I open that door.

The short answer is that I want to meet my birth family, but that just doesn't do it justice. 'I want to meet my father' has a little more weight, but even that doesn't remotely cover things. It's not just about some sort of narcissistic need to look in the eyes of someone who looks like you, it's about knowing what it feels like to hold and be held by a blood relative, to have that certainty of fact that no matter what happens, this person will always be related to you. It's simple things that everyone else takes for granted, like being able to look in a mirror and know you have your father's eyes and your mother's lips. Or being able to look at a nephew or niece and picture what your own children might look like. Or knowing that your family has a medical history of, well, of anything at all. Imagine what it's like to never have seen another woman or man from your own family. To not know what a teenager with your genes looks like until you turn into one. To not know if you're more likely to be fat than thin, tall rather than short. To wonder how you will grow old. To spend your life looking for clues in the faces of strangers with a similar colouring or body shape.

But it's not just a physiological curiosity, it's not knowing anything about where you've come from, having no history with which to align yourself – it's like floating in the ocean without an anchor. Nowhere is this better demonstrated than by the fact that, once they are handed over to their new parents, adopted children are often stripped of any last detail of their past that might remain. I was lucky, my parents kept my birth name as my middle name, always made sure it was there, waiting in the wings for whenever I wanted it. And although they gave me a new name too, they made sure it was one that would work in Eritrea as well as in England. They kept all my options open. But I know several adoptees who weren't just given new first names by their new parents, but were led to believe either that their birth parents never bothered to name them, or that the name they have always answered to is the one thing they have left from their first life. And then, as they start to trace, they discover they don't even have that.

Changing a child's name without telling them is stealing from them; it's as if you are trying to wipe out their history. And imagine what it does to you to discover in adulthood that the name you have now was a completely different one to the one you were first given. It's supposed to represent a fresh start in life, wiping the slate clean, but whose benefit is the new name for? And what does it really achieve except allowing the new parents to have a little Freddie like they always wanted, never mind that the child was originally called something else?

But there was only so long that knowing my name would be enough for me. Over the years, I have become more and more agitated by my adoption, more and more desperate to find whatever information about my past that I could. It has become an itch, a scab that I simply have to pick, no matter if it makes things worse instead of better. That is why, when I hear an adopted person swear blind that they don't have any wish to trace their birth family, I know they are lying. I know, because that used to be my lie. 'I'm lucky,' I used to say, 'I have a great adoptive family, so I don't need to trace.' I would almost believe myself. Just like I would almost feel pity for those adoptees I knew who had traced their birth families, with varying degrees of success. I wasn't one of those weirdos who could think of nothing but their adoption, who blamed everything that ever went wrong in their lives on the fact they were adopted. Not me. I was fine, I was great, and I didn't need all that stuff. Except I wasn't fine. I was just a very good liar. But while I may have had everyone else fooled, I couldn't fool myself. I knew it was only a matter of time before I came here. Even as a child, I knew it was a question of when, rather than if, and the reason I knew was because there was one question I couldn't get out of my head. It's the one question that all those other, smaller things boil down to. It's the simplest and yet it's the most painful to ask: 'Why did you give me away?'

The need to ask this question has simmered away for the best part of thirty years, and now it's finally boiled over. I can ignore it no longer, and it's at the heart of why so many adoptees go in search of their birth parents, no matter how wonderful, or otherwise, their adoptive families have been. And despite the fact that being rejected by their parents for a second time is the thing in the world that scares them the most. We all need to know why we were given up for adoption. If the fear of a repeated rejection is massive, then it goes to show how unstoppable the force of the desire to have this question answered is that so many adoptees are prepared to take the risk.

But it's not the rational, sensible 'why' that we want answered, not the 'better chance in life' explanation that we may have been fobbed off with all our lives, but the emotional, heartfelt 'why': Why didn't you want me? How could you do that to me? How could you leave me to fend for myself with complete strangers? Was I really so much trouble?

It is no coincidence that I know a lot of adopted adults. We have a habit of gravitating towards each other so, as the saying goes, some of my best friends are adopted. And yet, even though I know more than most, I have never heard the words, 'I am glad I was adopted.' Many are happy with the result, glad they got the adoptive parents they did, but not one person doesn't wish it hadn't happened in the first place. No matter how much love we may have for our adoptive parents, no matter how much we don't want to hurt them or how guilty we feel for having these thoughts, we all wish we hadn't been put up for adoption. My mother died. My father was a farmer in a village, who was left, I now knew, with five other children plus a newborn. He couldn't look after me and work the land. So he put me in an orphanage. Because of this one decision he made, my life took a completely different course. Unlike the rest of my birth family, I have never gone truly hungry, I have never prayed for rain, and I have never been displaced by war. I have a wonderful adoptive family, a brother and sister I adore, a job I love, a flat in one of the world's most expensive capitals – in fact all the trappings of Western success. Looking at the facts, if anyone should be relieved to have been adopted, it should be me. My adoption has meant I escaped terrible hardships and the likelihood of early death. Even I know that a motherless child does not last long in the villages. Had I not been placed in that orphanage, assuming I made it past infancy, I would have had a normal Eritrean peasant girl's life – complete with a stint on the front doing my national service, an arranged marriage, and children in my teens. But I still wish none of it had happened, I still wish I had never been adopted, and, most importantly, I still want to know, 'Why? Why me?'

And now, here I am, on one side of a door, with the only people who can answer that question on the other. If I listen I can probably hear them speaking. I wonder what they are saying; I wonder what they are thinking. Do they sense I am outside the door? Isn't that what blood relatives do, sense each other's presence?

Under my breath I whisper the few words of Tigrinya Gaim taught me, so that I would at least be able to greet my father in his own language. And then I look to Manna and nod that I am ready for him to knock on the door. As soon as he knocks I want to run, run as fast and as far away from here as possible, not looking behind until I am a safe distance away – the hotel perhaps, or the airport? In that one knock, that one moment, I feel as if I have lost what little power I had left in this process. He has knocked on the door, and unless I run away, it is inevitable I will meet my family. It's not that the desire to meet them has suddenly vanished, it's just that it has finally gone beyond the point of no return. It is one thing to spend your whole adult life wanting to meet your family, it is quite another to know it will be happening in a matter of seconds and there is nothing you can do about it. I glance up the dirt track to see if there is an obvious escape route. There isn't, and besides it's not as if they don't know where I am staying. I silently urge Manna to see the fear in my face, but to no avail. I can hear someone behind the door, shunting the lock to one side. A short man with blue-black skin, a round face and a very white moustache opens the door. Is he my father, I wonder? Should I hug him? He looks nothing like me, but then what was I expecting, a body double? Maybe I get my looks from my mother and my brains from him?

Just as I'm about to take a gamble and lunge at him, he says hello to me, in English, and motions me towards a court-yard that is behind the door. 'Come, come,' he says, his eyes twinkling behind a pair of tinted glasses. 'Everyone is inside. They are very excited to meet you.'

I walk through the courtyard, trying not to step on a couple of small children who have appeared from nowhere. In the middle of the courtyard is a mango tree, heavy with fruit. 'Wow, mangoes on trees!' I hear myself say, to no one in particular, like the tourist I am. It doesn't matter, as no one replies and I am pushed towards yet another door.

'I will open the door,' says Manna, 'and then you will walk in.' And with that, he reaches in front of me with his right arm and gently pushes open the door. I stand there rooted to the spot as his arm sweeps forwards.

'Oh my God, he's opening the sodding door,' is all I can think. I feel him give me a gentle shove.

11

I step into the room, and as my eyes adjust to the light, I hear a collective gasp. And then it begins, a high-pitched ululating 'Lelelelelelelele'. Standing in front of me are five people, four men and one woman. I am busy trying to find the oldest man, figuring he will be my father and that I should greet him first, when they all move forward and encircle me. Everyone is hugging. I realize the noise has changed. Every single person in the room, apart from me, is now crying. The circle breaks and someone pushes me towards an old, frail-looking man, who must be my father, but I am having trouble focusing on just one person. The old man squeezes me tightly. And then he starts to sob. All I can think is how thin he is. I can feel his ribs. I wonder if he can feel my fat? He pulls away, brings his hands up to my face, and starts to kiss me on alternate cheeks, and in between kisses he takes his hands from my face and holds them above his head and says the same word, *'Yemesgin'*, over and over again. I have no idea what he is saying, but it seems to warrant a response. I decide to try out what little Tigrinya I know: *'Kemelehey?'* (How are you?) I ask.

The room gasps again. My father is the first to recover: *'Tsbuk,'* (I'm good) he says, solemnly, then *'Tsbuk'* again.

He then says the phrase back to me, and I reply, *'Tsbuk.'*

The atmosphere is expectant. Everyone is standing in silence, and I'm not sure whether they are dazed or confused. Eventually my father starts to speak. I have no idea what he is saying, so I just listen to his gravelly voice and the sing-song of his words. Every so often I sort of nod in agreement. He comes to a stop and I feel everyone's eyes turn to me. He repeats the last phrase, and starts to jab me in my chest. I apologetically shake my head and say, in English, 'I'm so sorry, I don't understand,' hoping that Manna or someone else in the room who speaks English will come to my rescue. He repeats the phrase again, this time jabbing himself and then me in the chest. I wonder if anyone else can see the funny side of this. It's like that sketch of an English person abroad: they don't speak the language but figure that if they speak English loudly enough locals will understand. Except if I were watching this scene, instead of taking part in it, I'd find it sad rather than funny.

Everyone is looking confused and it suddenly dawns on me why. By greeting my father in Tigrinya, I've given the impression I can speak the language, when all I know is one or two phrases. As soon as I click, I feel like a complete con merchant. They probably never dreamt for a moment that I'd speak Tigrinya, and then I came in with one phrase and got their hopes up, only to dash them again within minutes. You know that dream where you're naked in front of the whole school or office? And that moment of panic as you realize what's wrong? That's what this feels like. They have seen through my clothes, or rather my pathetic attempts to fit in, to please, and here I stand completely naked, exposed for the bogus Eritrean I am. It would be funny if it weren't so tragic. The room is silent; no one seems to know what to do next.

A young man in his early thirties, with dark skin, a small moustache and delicate features, wearing a denim shirt and jeans, steps forward. 'We are all very happy to meet you,' says the man, in perfect English, holding out his hand. I hold mine out, trying not to show the huge extent of my relief at having someone speak to me in English. He grabs hold of my hand, and then pulls me towards him, and as he hugs me he starts to cry. He then holds my face and starts kissing me on alternate cheeks. I stand there focusing all my energy on not tensing up or flinching. I have never been very good at public displays of anything, especially emotion. When he is done, after what seems like an age but is probably only a few minutes, he breaks away. I only just catch my breath when someone else grabs hold of me and hugs me to them. I don't even get a chance to see what this person looks like, such is the speed and force with which they hug me. This is how it goes on for the best part of half an hour. I am passed, like a parcel, around the room, each person in turn hugging me, kissing me and crying, then passing me on to the next. I feel no emotion, only a sense of bewilderment, confusion, and vague annoyance at being mauled. This is not how I had pictured things – everyone else overcome with emotion, and me standing there feeling numb. Why aren't I crying? I will the tears to come, but nothing happens. I used to be able to make myself cry just imagining this moment, and now here I am going right through it and nothing, not a single drop.

All I feel is numb. I've felt more emotionally involved watching *EastEnders*. Maybe I'm just too freaked out to cry. Maybe I could stoke up a little emotion if it didn't feel like there was already more than enough in the room. I've seen enough reunions on daytime television to expect some tears, but not this outpouring. I want it to stop. All this crying feels like it's getting in the way, though of what I'm not sure. I want to tell them to stop but I can't even do that. I can barely get a look at everyone's faces with all this crying. And as for the hugging? Well I'd probably relax a bit more if that stopped too. The only time I let this many people touch me is on the Central Line, and even then it's hardly through choice. I hate to say it, but I never realized how English I was. Right now, I'd kill for some good old-fashioned stiff upper lips. All this emotion is weirding me out, making me feel like some sort of non-crying alien in a world of teary folk. Not only can I not speak their language, I can't even cry with them.

Are they looking at me, wondering why I'm not crying? I must be making a really bad impression. I bet they're thinking I'm a right heartless cow. 'She's meeting us for the first time and she looks like she doesn't give a toss,' is probably what they are thinking, assuming there's a Tigrinya word for 'toss'. And they'd be right. Not about the not giving a toss bit, but, well, how can I be expected to cry when I haven't got a clue what's going on around me? And if this outpouring of emotion is meant to make me feel welcome, it's having the opposite effect. I feel like I can't very well start crying too because, well, because then we'd all be crying and where would it end? Someone in the room has to keep it together, keep it from getting too weird, and I guess that person is me. Besides, I don't really know what they are crying about or for. It's not as if they've ever met me before or didn't know I was coming. I could be anyone. In fact, it feels as if anyone could have walked into the room at that moment and they'd all have started crying. It all feels a bit false, staged, disingenuous somehow. All this emotion is too much too soon. How can you cry that much over someone you've never met? I am a stranger to them, and yet here they are, crying like I'm their closest friend. And besides, if they're that upset, then why did they give me up for adoption? What's the crying supposed to do other than make me feel bad? It's as if I've made them cry, and I can't figure out if it's because I waited so long – relief-crying – or because they are happy I came at all. It's as if because I'm the only one not crying, then the fact they are must be my fault. I just wish they'd all stop because it's making me feel bad. And it's putting up a wall between us: they're crying, I'm not. I can feel myself getting impatient. I've got things I want to say, questions I want to ask, but I can't get near any of them with all this crying.

I have now been hugged, kissed, and cried over by everyone in the room, but not actually introduced to anyone by name. I am gently shoved towards my father again (my father!); he holds my face in his hands and starts to speak. The room is quiet, except for the low, solemn sound of his voice, and the occasional sob from someone else. Every so often, someone will gasp, raise one or two hands and say something towards the sky, not quite interrupting, but more in agreement with whatever it is he's saying. As I have no clue what that is, but sense the gravity of the moment, I look into his eyes and take this opportunity to look at him close up.

His skin is a darker, richer brown than mine, but only by one or two shades. Is that the colour I would be if I lived here? He is not quite bald, but what hair he has is grey and cut in a close crop to his small, elegantly shaped head. But it's the shape of his face that stops me in my tracks. Now I've started looking I can't stop. His face is exactly the same shape as mine. Exactly. His is thinner, considerably older, but the actual shape, the high forehead, large, slightly sunken eyes and the razor-sharp cheekbones – I've seen it all before in the mirror.

'He is thanking God for bringing you back to us,' says the denim-clad younger man. 'It is a true miracle.'

'Yes,' I say, nodding enthusiastically, feeling the sentiment, if not the religious symbolism.

'He is saying he will always be grateful to God for this miracle,' says the man.

Blimey, I think, how's an atheist supposed to respond to that one without dampening the mood? 'Oh, right, yeah, um, nice one,' I say, instantly regretting it. 'Nice one'? Where the hell did that come from? What the hell kind of thing is that to say to the father you met only moments ago? I'm in the middle of what will surely be one of the most emotional events of my life and all I can come up with is 'nice one'? It's hardly fitting for the occasion. Still, at least it's memorable.

Hoping that the unbearable naffness of the phrase will get lost in translation, I zone back in to my father, who is still speaking. 'He is saying he never thought he would live to see this day, but now he can die a happy man. God has given him back a daughter. Now he can rest in peace. If he died tomorrow, he would die satisfied.'

I guess I'm the only atheist in the room then. I can feel yet more walls going up with every mention of God. First the crying and all the touchy-feely stuff, and now this? I want to say that Lufthansa brought me here, not God, and that if he was so great, then why did God separate us in the first place? I want to say that God is a load of old bollocks, designed to make people feel better about their miserable lives, and that anyone who thanks him for anything is a mug. I want to say that I came here, me, on my own, without help from any divine being. I did this all by myself, I made it happen. I want to say God didn't take me away, you gave me up. I want to say all those things, and more, but instead I just nod, smile as enthusiastically as possible, and look vaguely towards the sky.

When my father finishes speaking, the man who was translating comes forward again. He is darker than the others, with a small round face instead of a pointy one. 'I am your brother, Medhanie,' he says, pointing to himself.

'Hello, Medhanie,' I say.

'Asrat,' he says, pointing to my father.

'Asrat,' says my father.

'Asrat,' I repeat dutifully.

'Stephanos,' says Medhanie, pointing to a slight, pretty man in army clothing, who looks so much like me I feel myself do a visible double take.

'Stephanos,' he says, pointing to himself.

'Stephanos,' I repeat.

'Zemichael,' says Medhanie, pointing to the youngest-looking man, who I recognize from the photograph that I've been carrying around for nearly ten years. His skin tone is lighter than everyone else's, in fact it's the same shade as my own. He spots this instantly and holds his arm against mine. Everyone in the room laughs, and I'm grateful for the light relief.

'Hi,' says Zemichael, 'it's good to meet you.'

'Zemichael, hi, it's good to meet you too. I still have your photograph,' I say.

'Ah yes, the letter, I am so glad I sent it.'

'And this,' says Medhanie, interrupting gently, 'is Timnit, your sister.'

She has the same colouring and face-shape as my father and Stephanos, but instead of looking solemn, she is grinning from ear to ear. We are standing opposite each other, so close I can feel her breath. 'I am standing in front of my sister!' I want to scream. It's as if everyone else in the room disappears, there's just me and Timnit. Two sisters, separated by a lifetime, standing opposite each other. I notice absent-mindedly that she is taller, just like Gaim said. Typical, I think. But that's not the thing I notice the most. The thing that is screaming back at me, the thing I can't get past, is the smile. Her smile. My smile.

A few moments pass, and then, for the first time since I walked into this room, I worry that I might burst into tears. There is a massive lump in my throat and I have absolutely no idea why. 'Timnit,' she says shyly, pointing to herself.

'Timnit,' I croak.

She then hugs me, kisses me again, and starts speaking. I can't tell if it's to me or to everyone else in the room, but when she finishes, she hugs me again, and then turns around and motions me to the green sofa I hadn't even noticed was behind us. There is a bit of a jostle to sit down, and eventually we are arranged so that I am in the middle, sandwiched between Timnit and my father, with the others sitting on either end. My father is holding one of my nervously limp, and by now very clammy hands, Timnit the other. My 'no hand holding on a first date' rule suddenly pops into my head. If only my friends could see me now.

As the room settles down, the conversation is thick and fast. Although I can't understand the Tigrinya, it's a safe bet that everyone is talking about me. I look to Medhanie for clues. He reads my look. 'They are discussing who you look the most like,' he says.

'Who do they say?' I ask. I have already decided that I have the colouring of Zemichael, a reddish brown compared to the others' deeper shade, and Timnit's smile, and that overall, I look most like Stephanos. I keep quiet: I want to know what they think.

'Well, you are the same colour as Zemichael,' (I smile and nod in agreement) 'but you look most like Himan.'

'Himan?' I say, confused. I don't remember being introduced to a Himan. Maybe I heard him wrong, maybe he said Hidat, my mother's name. 'Hidat, my mother, is that who I look like?' I say, just to be sure.

'No, Timnit looks most like Hidat; you look like *Himan*,' he says, stressing the first syllable.

By now I am completely baffled. 'I'm so sorry, I didn't catch who Himan was,' I say, looking around the room for someone I have missed. There is a short pause. Everyone looks to their feet, and then to my father. He says something to Medhanie and motions for him to tell me what he has just said.

'*U-we, u-we*,' says Medhanie, which I know means 'Yes, yes'. 'Ah, sorry, of course, you don't know. Himan was our sister, your sister, she died on the front in 1984 when she was about seventeen; that is who you look like.'

12

I have to get out of this room immediately. The walls are closing in and I need to get some fresh air. I can't take in this new information in front of all these people; it's too much to deal with in front of an audience, too many eyes wanting me to smile and act like I'm OK with it. I feel dizzy and I have a tightness in my throat that I know means I am either going to faint, vomit or dissolve into a puddle of tears.

Before I came here I was desperate to look like someone. I have spent my entire life wanting to look like someone, and, more importantly, wanting to know who that someone is. And now I know: I look like the dead sister I never knew I had. No wonder my father was thanking God. The daughter you've never seen walks in looking like the one you lost to the Struggle. That would probably make even me think there was a divine being.

Everyone is chatting around me, and I get the impression that the topic of conversation has moved on, that it would be wrong to ask them about Himan, that now is not the time, that it has all been dealt with years ago – that I've come into the conversation too late to have the right to contribute.

I excuse myself and ask for the bathroom. I lock the door and then stand over the toilet and dry retch a couple of times. Nothing much happens but I feel a bit better. I sit on the seat and start to sob silently. I don't really know what I'm crying about – is it for her, because she's dead, or is it for

myself, because I will never get to see her face to face? A
bit of both, I decide, hating myself for how selfish it makes
me feel: she's dead, and all I'm thinking about is how it
affects me.

I have lived my life knowing I would never meet my
mother. I mourn her, in my own way, regularly. But now
there is someone else I have lost. Within seconds of gaining a
sister, I have lost one. It's as if she has turned to dust just
before I could reach out and touch her. As soon as her name
was spoken, she was gone. The time between the words 'You
look like Himan' and 'she died on the front' is all I had her
for. And now, on what should be a wonderfully happy day, a
day about reunion, I am being denied something, someone,
yet again. My sadness quickly turns to anger. It's just typical
of my life. I can't look like my father, or my brother – oh no,
I have to look like my dead sister. The only person, other than
my mother, that I will never be able to meet.

After a few more minutes I start to feel better, stronger.
I splash my face several times with cold water, take a deep
breath and head back across the courtyard, past the mango
tree which seems to have lost all its allure, and back into the
room. No one seems to have noticed my funny turn, for which
I am grateful, so I sit back down on the sofa. I am just thinking
how much I could use a drink right now, a shot of something
strong, whisky or whatever it is you're supposed to have when
you're in shock, when I notice that in my absence someone
has placed a very small glass of clear liquid on the coffee table
in front of where I am sitting. 'If there is a God, then let that
be alcohol,' I think to myself. I look around and everyone is
holding up their tiny glasses. My father says something partly
skywards, partly in my general direction. A toast, using short

glasses full of clear liquid? It's got to be alcohol, got to be. Everyone murmurs in agreement when my father is finished, and then they go to drink. I knock the drink back and hope for the best. The slight burn in my throat, followed by that familiar warm sensation, is instantly recognizable. This must be Asmara gin, the Eritrean ouzo-like spirit I'd read about. I silently thank the very God I don't believe in. It is only when I put the glass down that I realize everyone is looking at me a bit oddly – well, more oddly than they were before. I look at their glasses and realize they all have most of their liquid left. Whoops. Just as I'm grasping at a straw and thinking that maybe they're all in awe of my shot-drinking capacity, I remember the bit in the guidebook about Eritrean women not really drinking alcohol. As I'm wondering what the Tigrinya is for 'I'm not an alcoholic, honest', Medhanie jumps to my rescue. 'You like it?' he says, kindly. 'It is *zabib*, an Eritrean drink, but you are supposed to just take a small amount.'

'It's lovely,' I say. My throat is still burning, but I'm still getting pleasure from a familiar sensation among all this madness. I'd really rather like another, but I sense once is a cultural transgression, twice would be bad form.

'Now we will eat, come and wash your hands,' says Medhanie, as everyone files out of the room. I join them and head back across the courtyard, relieved to be back out in the fresh air.

'Usually, because you are a girl, and the youngest, you would wash last, but today, because it is a special day, you shall wash after our father,' says Zemichael.

As we file back into the room one of the older women, who seemed to sneak into the room after the main introductions, brings out a large round silver tray.

I ask Medhanie who she is, and he tells me she is Zerai's wife, Tiebe.

'Who is Zerai?' I ask, getting more confused.

'He is your cousin,' says Medhanie, patiently.

'But who is he?' I ask exasperatedly.

'He is the son of your father's sister,' replies Medhanie.

And then I click. 'Is he the man with the sparkly eyes?'

'Yes,' says Medhanie, laughing at my description of our cousin.

Covering the tray is an *injera*, the greyish, thin, spongy, pancake-like bread that forms a main part of the Eritrean diet. Timnit comes into the room and ladles some meat in a juicy-looking blood-orange-coloured sauce into piles around the *injera*. A young girl – who I've only just noticed, perhaps she's Zerai and Tiebe's daughter – comes in and spoons another sort of stew on to the remaining bread. I am the only woman not helping to serve the food. I wonder if it is my newness or my Westernness that has elevated me to the status of honorary male? Once the novelty wears off, will I be expected to fetch and carry the food in a way the men are obviously not? As I am wondering, Tiebe comes back in with another tray, this one loaded with rolled-up *injera*. Zerai breaks off several pieces of *injera* and hands them around. I thank him for mine, and am just about to have a little nibble, when he bows his head and starts to speak. Shit, I think, they're praying before they eat. Thank God I didn't just start troughing away. I too bow my head, and wait until I hear what sounds like an 'amen'.

'Eat, eat,' says Medhanie. I suddenly realize how hungry I am, and start to tuck in. Just as I'm thinking what a relief it is to have everyone focused on eating, rather than on me, my father turns to me with a handful of food in one hand and, saying something in Tigrinya, points towards my mouth with the other. Once again, I have no idea what he is saying, so I just sort of smile and nod in appreciation of the food. Then he points at me again. 'He wants to feed you,' says Medhanie.

'Feed me?' I ask, not sure what Medhanie means.

'It's a way to celebrate, to show love, to feed someone from your own hand,' he replies. All eyes are on me, but I still don't really know what I am supposed to do. 'Just open your mouth and he will feed you,' says Medhanie, as if trying to persuade a small child. I do as he says and hope my hesitation doesn't come across as unwillingness. As my father brings his right hand up and gently eases the food into my mouth with his fingers, I see his eyes have welled up. The moment feels almost too intimate. A communal ripple of relief goes around the room and the tension is broken. Someone taps me on my shoulder. I turn around and see Timnit, with food in her hand. I open my mouth, the food goes in, and this time everyone cheers and claps. This happens three more times, until all my brothers have also fed me. Then others start feeding each other – Timnit feeds my father, Medhanie feeds Zemichael, and so on. By this stage, I'm starting to feel full, but there is no let up. I feel bad enough refusing a second helping when I go to someone's house for dinner, but it's impossible to shake your head when someone is offering you food from their own hand. It's a dieter's nightmare: how on earth are you supposed to be able to tell how many calories you're eating? And are you allowed to say, 'Actually, I'm on Atkins at the moment, can you just give me the meat?' Even when people have stopped feeding me and each other, every time I pause for breath someone starts telling me to eat, like some sort of bad

Woody Allen Jewish-mother cliché. I take to holding a glass of water to my mouth, so that each time it looks as if someone is about to say, 'Eat, eat,' I take a sip and they don't say a word. It's a trick I read about years ago in an article about anorexics.

When dinner is over the women clear everything away, but I am told to sit down when I try to help. Then Tiebe comes back into the room and sets up a tiny metal stove in the corner. It's time for coffee.

There is nothing quite like Eritrean coffee. Apart from, perhaps, Ethiopian coffee, but that's for someone else's book. Eritrean coffee and, more importantly, the ceremony that goes with it make a quick cup of Nescafé look like sacrilege. I'm not really a coffee drinker, never have been, but Eritrean coffee is where I make an exception, and it's not out of some misguided sense of loyalty. It's because it tastes so damn good. Served in small cups (called *finjal*) that look like porcelain shot glasses, Eritrean coffee is as thick as it is sweet – your host will automatically put three sugars in the tiny cups; you are welcome to have more. But it's in the making of the coffee that the real ceremony lies. The host, always a woman, sits on a low stool over a small tin stove. Once the charcoal is fully stoked, she takes a couple of handfuls of fresh beans and roasts them over the fire in a metal can (a *fernello*) that looks like a very deep, square ladle. When the beans are fully roasted (they're heated at least three times), she walks around the room with the ladle, and everyone wafts the smoke of the beans in their direction, savouring the delicious smell. Returning to the stove, she places the coffee pot on top of it, crushing the beans with a pestle while the water in the pot heats up. The crushed beans are then transferred to the waiting pot, which is brought to the boil. The whole process takes at least half an hour. But that's not all. Being invited for coffee in someone's home is an honour, and accepting is something of a commitment, for it is considered bad luck to have anything less than three cups. And more often than not, you'll be served with popcorn as well.

As the coffee cups come around, I sit there musing that if there was ever a time when I didn't need a caffeine high, now was probably it. But I know how rude it would be to refuse, so I drink my coffee, munch on some popcorn and sit there politely. My cheeks are beginning to hurt from all this smiling. So is my head. Suddenly I have had enough. It's too much – all these people, all this emotion in one room. I can't relax or get a sense of anyone because I'm too busy trying to make sure I don't cause offence or ruin this day for them. It's fine for them, they have each other; but I am in a room full of strangers. All I want to do is go back to my hotel room and shut the door on the rest of the world. I've got so much stuff swilling around my head that it feels as if it's about to explode. And now I am going to get all hyper because of the coffee, not to mention the gallon of sugar that comes with it. I wonder what my escape plan should be. I know I have to stay for at least three cups, but does that mean I can start making 'I need to leave' noises after two? What reason shall I give? I'm tired? I have a headache? Perhaps both? I take my third cup of syrupy coffee and think how much I just want to go to sleep. It's the only way I can imagine my head will stop buzzing. I'm sure everything will seem less overwhelming in the morning, but right now, I need to be on my own.

Medhanie stands up as if to make an important announcement. 'Please don't let it be anything major,' I think. I don't think I can take any more revelations this evening. 'Now we will go into town and leave the elders to rest,' he says.

Thank God for that, I think, trying hard not to let my face show my relief. I concentrate what energies I have left on not rushing through the goodbyes. I thank Zerai and Tiebe for dinner and coffee, and I promise everyone, several times over, that I will return tomorrow. Stephanos and Zemichael are also saying their goodbyes, but Timnit doesn't seem to be going anywhere. I ask her, in English, if she is coming with us. She shakes her head. 'Why not?' I ask. She laughs, puts her hands into a prayer position, and puts them against the left side of her cheek, closing her eyes and bending her head to the left as she does so. 'Ah, you're tired?' I say, copying her actions. She nods her head vigorously. 'Me too,' I say, exaggerating a fake yawn and pointing to myself. She grabs both my hands and we both start to laugh. It is the first joke I have shared with my sister.

13

Once outside the house, I feel myself perk up, the weight of emotion in there lifted off my shoulders. Medhanie hails a yellow cab and we pile in. 'I am in a taxi with my brothers' is all I can think. I want to say it out loud, but as it's not a sentence I ever expected to say I don't want to jinx the moment.

'Do you want to go back to your hotel, or would you like to go for a walk and maybe a Coke?' says Medhanie.

'Well, I am in a taxi with my brothers for the first time ever,' I venture, unable to keep the thought in, 'I think we should celebrate.' All three laugh, even Stephanos, who I know doesn't speak English, but more than makes up for it by looking so much like me. As we get into town, we bundle out of the taxi and start to stroll along Liberation Avenue. There are still plenty of people on the streets, and I'm glad of the distraction. We walk the length of the road and turn around to go back down in the other direction. As we pass a café with chairs outside, Zemichael asks if I'd like to sit down and have a drink. Desperate as I am for a shot of something strong I think I should wait until I'm at the hotel, so I ask what he's having. 'I will have a Sprite,' he says.

'Then so will I,' I reply, with as much enthusiasm as I can muster.

Medhanie says he'll have a Coke, and then, in Tigrinya, asks Stephanos what he'd like. Zemichael and Medhanie laugh at Stephanos' reply.

'What is he having?' I ask.

'He wants a whisky,' says Medhanie, smiling.

I laugh, thinking perhaps it's alcohol, rather than blood, that is thicker than water. 'I'd love a whisky too,' I say, emboldened by Stephanos' request.

Medhanie and Zemichael raise their eyebrows but ask the waitress nonetheless. 'They don't have any, but there's Asmara beer?' says Medhanie.

'Sure, a beer would be lovely,' I say.

Medhanie tells Stephanos that I am joining him in the beer, and he laughs and nods his head in approval.

As we sit in the warmth of the early evening, my brothers talk among themselves, occasionally turning to me and checking I am OK. I sit there, enjoying being left alone, sipping my beer and thinking that perhaps things aren't so bad, so weird, after all. Maybe this is all it comes down to: sitting in the warm evening breeze drinking beer with my brothers.

Two beers later and tiredness comes crashing over me. The beer and the fresh air have given me a sense of calm, taken the edge off the evening's events and the three coffees. My desire to be on my own has returned, though this time it's less manic. I am just about to make my excuses when Zemichael does a little stretch, as if to tell me it's OK if I want to call it a night.

'Are you tired?' I ask.

'Yes, I think we all are. It is only early, but so much happened today that we need to go and rest, don't you think?' he says.

'Yes, definitely,' I say, hoping he can hear how grateful I am for his lifeline.

As we walk back to my hotel, a comfortable silence falls upon us. We say goodbye in the lobby, and make arrangements for them to meet me here in the morning. I get my key and head for my room. As I close the door and lean against it, I let out a massive sigh: 'I did it,' I whisper. And then the tears come.

I slide down the door, curl up on the hard floor and cry as I have never cried before, and as I am doing so, I hope nothing will ever make me cry like this again. I let everything out: all the sadness and the anger I have ever felt about being adopted. I cry for my mother and the sister I have only just learnt I had, neither of whom I will ever meet; I cry for the years I spent wondering about my birth family. I cry for the hard life that shows on my father's face, and the first ever joke I shared with my sister. I cry for my dad in England and how me coming here might have made him feel, and for Tom and Lydia and how they might feel when they learn I have three other brothers and a sister who look like me. I cry at how complicated and insurmountable it all seems. I cry with joy and I cry with relief, but mostly I cry at how alone I felt in that room in Mai Tameni, despite the fact that I finally had everything I have ever wanted.

Are these the tears that wouldn't come earlier, I think? I stop trying to think about why I am crying, and just let myself give in to it. I'm not really sure how long I sit on the floor crying – ten minutes, maybe twenty – but eventually the sobs stop, as does the shaking. I go from crying to snivelling, and as I'm not really a snivelling sort, I decide enough is enough and go to the bathroom to see the damage I have done to my capillaries. I splash cold water on my face and remember I've got some eye gel somewhere. I knew it would come in handy. I apply the cream and start to potter around the room. I am restless with that strange sense of post-crying euphoria, so

I decide that the best thing for it is to go down to the hotel bar and order a glass of wine and a packet of cigarettes. The wine comes, but I have inadvertently ordered a bottle. Never mind, I think, I'll just have a glass now and save the rest. I light a cigarette, pour a glass of wine and sit in the bar for a few moments. Despite the wine and the cigarettes, or maybe because of them, it isn't long before I start to feel uncomfortable. I look around and realize people are looking me up and down. I then realize that here, in this relatively up-market hotel, an Eritrean woman drinking and smoking by herself usually only means one thing. Normally I would stay sitting there to make a point, staging my own personal rebellion, but not tonight. I am too tired for any sort of rebellion, no matter how small. So I stub out my cigarette, take the rest of my wine, and head upstairs to sit on my balcony. I grab my Walkman off the bedside table and then I sit on the balcony for a good hour, just gazing out across the city, wondering what to make of it all. I don't cry again, and in fact the numbness has come back. I keep asking myself how I feel, and I can't seem to find the answer. But I realize now that it's not because I feel nothing, it's because I feel so much. Exhausted, and hoping sleep will give me clarity, I go to bed wondering what it will feel like to wake up as a different person.

14

As soon as I open my eyes it hits me: yesterday I met my family. There isn't even a second of doubt or of the 'where am I?' confusion that I usually get when I wake in un-familiar surroundings. It's as if I've not really been asleep. Sure, sleep came, and when it did it was deep, but I wake with a start of realization that yesterday was the big day. It's over.

I did it. I have done it. Do I feel different? I'm not really sure. I certainly feel something, but that might just be a murky head from the bottle of wine I polished off. I get up, walk into the bathroom and stand in front of the mirror. Well, I don't look any different, which is kind of disappointing. I'm not entirely sure how I expected my appearance to change, and I didn't even realize that I did expect it to until just a few seconds ago, but now that I think about it, some sort of tangible difference, a before and after if you like, would have been nice. An instant radiance perhaps, or some other visible sign of the weight that has finally been lifted from my shoulders. A few extra inches wouldn't go amiss. Nothing major, just the kind of thing that makes people ask if you've just had your hair cut or lost some weight. But no, I look exactly the same, in fact if anything I look worse than I did yesterday, thanks to my hangover skin and puffy eyes from all that crying. Still, they'd be a darn sight worse had it not been for the eye gel, and I might not know how I'm feeling but I do know how to hide a heavy night. I look at my watch. It's 8.30 and my brothers are coming to pick me up at nine, so I'd better get a move on. I slather on a moisturising face mask, take pleasure in the fact I am at least as vain as I was yesterday, and jump in the shower. A few minutes later the hangover has shifted and any signs of last night's excesses or tears have gone with it. I'm not sure why, but I really don't want my brothers to know I've been crying.

I go to the wardrobe and pull out the long linen dress I rejected last night. I still wouldn't be seen dead in it at home, but I suppose I should make an effort to at least look like the ideal daughter. And besides, my dad always loves it when I wear dresses, and I bet dads pretty much the world over are the same when it comes to seeing their daughters in dresses. I pull the dress on, and instantly feel out of sorts. I look, and feel, like I'm wearing a potato sack. What on earth possessed me to buy this thing? I know it said in the guidebook that dresses and skirts had to be long and not tight and show absolutely nothing resembling a cleavage, but surely it's just as offensive to be in horrid clothes as it is to be in revealing ones? Not even my dad would like this particular number. I slip on my Birkenstocks, which just add insult to injury, and head out of the room, only mildly amused at the irony of it all. I hardly ever wear dresses at home, and when I do, I compensate for their girliness by making sure they are either short, low cut or tight, and frequently all three. And now, here I am, walking out of the door in something I would not only have shunned but probably fallen about laughing had anyone ever suggested I'd consider it for my wardrobe at home. Oh well, it's not as if anyone around here knows me.

I go downstairs and there they are: my brothers, sitting on

the green sofas in the lobby. Thankfully they look as sheepish as I feel.

'Hello my sister, did you sleep well?' says Medhanie, jumping up. I can't help but smile at the attempt at small talk, the effect of which he's blown instantly by his use of the word sister.

'Um, yes, very well, thank you. I fell asleep as soon as you left me,' I lie. Well, 'Not really, I was up half the night either drinking wine or crying. How about you?' wouldn't be fair, would it?

'We could not sleep at all, we were thinking about you all night,' says Zemichael. Oh great, now I've given them the impression I didn't give them a moment's thought. 'We should go now; people are waiting for us at the house in Mai Tameni.'

As we step outside into the sunshine they jostle, each one of them trying to stand next to me. I'm almost overwhelmed by how special it makes me feel. Zemichael is to my right, Medhanie to my left and Stephanos is in front of us, turning around with the conversation. I wonder if I'll ever get used to this, if walking down the road with my brothers will ever feel normal. I spot a phone booth across the road, and as I do I suddenly feel terribly guilty as I realize I haven't called my dad since the day after I arrived. In fact, the last contact I had with him was an e-mail I sent when I'd been here a couple of days, when I was still in holiday mode.

'Did you call your family in England last night?' says Zemichael, reading my mind.

'Yes,' I say, bold as brass, hoping they can't hear the guilt in my voice. I don't know why I didn't call my dad, and I don't know why I just lied to my brothers about it, but I do know the two are connected.

119

Why didn't I call my dad? I can't even say I meant to. It's not that I didn't think about it, but more that I made a conscious decision not to, which is why I now feel so bad. I was just so churned up inside, I had no idea what I was feeling – happy or sad, emotional or numb. I simply didn't think I'd be able to articulate my feelings, or rather police my words, which meant I might have said something to upset him. The thought of hurting my dad is one of the things that made coming here so hard, and I knew that he'd analyse every word of the conversation. I just couldn't trust myself. It seemed easier to not call at all than call and risk saying something insensitive – I felt the same as I did the night I came back from meeting my cousin, but much, much worse. But I don't want my brothers to know this. It's suddenly really important that they think my dad and I are rock solid, that he is there for me no matter what, and that of course I called him after the scariest day of my life. After all, what would it say about us if I hadn't called him? And as for lying to my brothers, well, I didn't want them to think I'm not close to my dad, and telling them I hadn't called would be like saying I didn't care about him, which couldn't be further from the truth. I didn't call because I care so much.

We hail a cab, pile in, and head back to the house we were at the evening before. 'Who is at the house?' I ask.

'It is a surprise, but today will be a very good day,' says Zemichael.

Christ, have I not had enough surprises for one holiday, I think to myself.

We get out of the taxi and walk the dusty track to the house. The entrance looks much less forbidding in the daylight, but otherwise it looks pretty much the same, apart from the goat tied to the gate. Medhanie sees me looking at the goat. 'Ah, that is for you,' he says.

'Excuse me?'

'The goat, it is for you, to celebrate that we have found you.'

'Oh, right, thanks,' I respond, contemplating vegetarianism for the first time in my life, and hoping, for my sake as much as the goat's, that he doesn't mean what I think he means. As I'm contemplating the goat's fate, the man with the twinkly eyes, whose name I have completely forgotten, opens the door. We walk through the courtyard and I take off my sunglasses, figuring it's probably a tad rude to meet long-lost relatives wearing shades – kind of like the sartorial equivalent of chewing gum.

I instantly regret taking them off as my sunglasses are actually prescription, which means that, as I haven't had time to put my regular glasses on, I can now barely see – but hopefully I'll be able to make out my immediate family. I squint my way into the room and to my horror it's much fuller than yesterday evening. As I walk in, everyone starts to clap and cheer, with the women ululating. I scour the room for my father, figuring that no matter who else is here I should greet him first. I spot him in a chair to my right and say hello, and he gets up, hugs me and kisses me three times on alternate cheeks. The room erupts with more cheering. He says something in Tigrinya. I turn to Medhanie and Zemichael for help. He says it again, pointing to his chest.

'Who is he?' says Medhanie.

I'm confused.

'He wants you to tell him who he is.'

'Oh, right.' I turn back to him: he wants me to tell the room he is my father, like a new father wanting their child to say

'Daddy' in front of his friends. Obviously I haven't a clue how to say that in Tigrinya, but I do at least know his name. 'Asrat,' I say, to the room as much as to him. There is a collective gasp, and then a definite cooling of the atmosphere. I turn to Medhanie. 'What? What is it?' I ask.

'That is Amehatzion, he is your uncle. Asrat, your father, is in the chair over there,' he points to a chair in the far left corner of the room. My father looks across at me, crestfallen, and says something, and though I can't understand a word he says, I'm pretty sure by the look of hurt on his face that it was along the lines of 'she doesn't even know her own father'.

My heart sinks. 'I'm so sorry,' I say, fumbling in my bag. 'It's not that I don't know you, it's just, well, I didn't have my glasses on,' I say, babbling away in English and pulling out the damned glasses and waving them around as if they're some sort of exhibit in a trial. Everyone is staring at me like I'm deranged. I put the glasses on my nose, do a ridiculously over-the-top double take between the two chairs, then turn to my father and say, 'Ah ha, Asrat!' The room is quiet for a second as everyone looks to my father for his reaction. 'U-we,' (Yes) he says.

My father steps forward, puts his right arm around me protectively, as if to let me know he has forgiven me, and takes my left hand in his. He leads me to his brother and says his name again: 'Amehatzion.'

'Amehatzion,' I repeat.

'He is your father's brother,' says Medhanie.

I look at him properly this time, wearing my glasses, and am relieved to see they do look remarkably similar – the same elegant face, the same sharp, sunken cheekbones, eyes as big as planets. They can't be more than a few years apart in age.

My uncle gives me another hug and more kisses. He then starts to say something, waving his hands between himself and my father. 'Yes, they are brothers,' I say. He shakes his head, wags his finger in front of me and repeats whatever it was he was saying, repeating the back and forth hand-waving. 'I'm sorry, I don't know what you are saying,' I reply.

'He wants you to tell him who is older, him or Asrat,' says Zemichael.

Oh great, I think, another chance for me to offend my father. I take another, closer, look at both men and can't get over how surreal it all seems. Here I am, standing in front of my father for the second time in my life, and his brother for the first, and I'm being asked to play parlour games. You'd think they could give me a bit of a break.

'Amehatzion,' I venture, not really sure of the answer, but figuring it's just better politically to pick out my uncle as the older man. Thankfully I'm right on both counts – Amehatzion is the older of the two, and the look of childish pleasure on my father's face tells me I may have made up for my earlier cock-up.

'Amehatzion, *u-we*, *u-we*,' says my father to the room, laughing.

As the laughter subsides, an elderly but breathtakingly beautiful woman who has been standing next to my uncle steps forward. She's tiny, with quite possibly the most lined face I have ever seen. It's the kind of face where people would say, 'Oh, she used to be really beautiful,' but in her case the lines are actually part of her beauty. She is wearing full traditional dress – a long layered dress with a white cotton shawl or *gabi* around her head and over her shoulders – and her forehead has a fading but still prominent tattooed cross, which means she must be ultra-Orthodox. She is also wearing a huge, welcoming smile.

'*Selam?*' I say – more as a question than a greeting. I want to ask her name, but have no idea how.

'*Selam. Merhaba, Merhaba,*' she replies.

Before I can ask one of my brothers what she is saying, her face crumbles, she throws her arms around me, and starts to cry. But something about this woman makes me not tense up. Unlike when the others were crying, I don't shake myself free too soon, and I almost don't even mind that much; in fact it feels kind of comfortable, her hugging me.

'This is your aunt,' says Zemichael, as soon as the woman lets me go. 'Her name is Rigbay; she is Amehatzion's wife.'

'Oh, thanks – can you tell her I'm very pleased to meet her,' I reply.

She turns around, sits down on the green sofa and pats the seat next to her, indicating for me to come and sit next to her. I walk over and join her. She picks up my hands, holds them and squeezes them several times, as if she can't believe I'm still sitting here. Her smile is back, and up close her honey-coloured face looks like a maze, the tattoo adding yet more mystery. She lets go of my left hand, lifts her right hand up to my face and starts to slowly stroke my right cheek. Then she strokes the other cheek, then my forehead, my eyes, even my nose. It's such a soft touch, like the kind of stroke someone gives you when they are telling you they love you. But I'm not freaked out. I like it. At one point I even close my eyes, just for a second. When I open them, hers are also closed. They spring open, she smiles at me staring at her lines, and starts to speak. Frustrated that I haven't a hope of understanding her, I turn to Zemichael, who I have decided is the more emotional of my two English-speaking brothers. He just seems to be more in tune with how alien and difficult this must all be for me. Maybe it's because he grew up in a children's home and had to rediscover his family when he left there at eighteen. He knows what it's like to feel like an outsider in your own family, in our family.

'She is telling you that she never thought this day would come. She can't believe you are here.'

I turn back to her and smile and nod, hoping I look like I get the magnitude of her feelings, but pretty sure I just look a bit simple.

'She says when you were a baby you suckled from her breast,' says Zemichael.

'What?' I reply, sure I can't have heard right.

'When our mother died, it was she who fed you. She is saying that at first you refused, you didn't take to her milk, but then later on you were hungry and you were fine. She was your mother's best friend, so when your mother died, she fed you for her, she gave you her milk. She wanted to keep you but couldn't because she had her own children to look after.'

This is the first time anyone has mentioned my mother, or the fact that she died so soon after giving birth to me. Hearing her spoken about by someone who knew her brings all the questions I have about her flooding to the surface. There is so much I want to know about my mother, but up to now I've felt like I didn't want to upset people by bringing her up. And now my aunt has done just that – talked about her and her death openly, as if giving me a green light to continue with that topic of conversation. 'What was she like?' I ask, jumping at the chance.

15

The trouble with the dead is that no one will speak ill of them. There are many reasons I have come here, a fair few of which I haven't gotten to the bottom of yet myself, but one of the things of which I was always certain was that I would finally learn what my mother was like – what kind of woman she was, and I guess, ultimately, whether I am like her in any way. Do I have any of her traits, despite the fact I never knew her? But whenever I ask anyone about her, so far all I have been met with is a series of platitudes: 'She was a lovely woman', 'She died very young' is about the size of it. And when I try and dig further – 'Yes, but what was she really like?' – all I get is confused looks, and more sentiment – 'I told you, she was a lovely woman.' How am I supposed to build up a picture of my mother based on that? Can they not see how hungry I am for something, anything, personal?

'What is she saying?' I ask my brothers, hoping they are not by now so tired of translating that they can't be bothered to do it fully.

'She is saying that our mother was her best friend, they were like sisters,' says Zemichael.

'Yes, but what was my mother actually like?'

'She was like her sister,' says Zemichael.

'I know that, but what was she like – her personality, what was it like?'

'I am sorry, I don't know what you want me to say?' says Zemichael, confused.

'Can you ask her if she remembers a story about my mother, something they did together, perhaps?' I ask, trying another tack.

Zemichael, looking relieved, turns and says some words to my aunt and turns back to me with her response. 'She remembers the day you were born, it was such a sad day, she says there is not a day when she doesn't miss Hidat.'

Everyone sitting around her on the sofa, myself included, goes quiet, and I sit there wishing I hadn't asked so many questions. A few minutes later, my father motions for me to sit next to him. Reluctantly I let go of my aunt's hand. I don't know why, but I felt more comfortable sitting next to her than anyone else in this new family of mine. The romantic in me thinks perhaps it's some sort of ancient muscle memory, triggered off by how she smells – my body knowing that this woman once fed me from her own breast. But more likely it's her overall warmth – and besides, when did I suddenly get all spiritual?

As I prepare to sit down next to my father he starts to tug almost anxiously at the skirt of my dress. 'Yes, I'm coming,' I say, sitting and smiling, worried that I have offended him by spending so much time with my aunt, or by plugging her for information about my mother, his dead wife. But as I sit, he gets more, not less, anxious. By now he's really tugging at my dress and waving his hands at me. Suddenly I get it, or at least I think I do. 'What is he saying?' I ask Medhanie, not wanting to jump to conclusions.

Medhanie is smiling, even though my father is not. 'What do you think he is saying?' he says.

'Well, I think there is a problem,' I say to Medhanie, who nods.

'Yes, you are quite right, there is a problem,' he says, his grin getting bigger.

'What is the problem?' I ask Medhanie, for the first time today thankful that no one else in earshot speaks English.

'What do you think the problem is?' asks Medhanie, still smirking, so I assume it's not too bad a transgression.

'Is it the length of my skirt?' I venture.

'Yes, it is,' he says, before being interrupted by our father. 'He wants to know why your skirt is so short.'

As I hastily apologize, and make vain attempts at pulling the skirt down towards my ankles, my father starts waving his hands in a similar fashion at my head. 'What is he saying now?' I ask Medhanie. Surely there can't be anything wrong with my hair? I have worn my hair in an Afro for nearly four years. Previously I shaved my head, but by 1999 I was bored with getting the clippers out every weekend, so I made growing my hair back my millennial new year's resolution – it is pretty much the only resolution I have ever kept first time around. The shaved head served me well, and though I bitterly denied it at the time, it was a protest of sorts against the way society expects black women to wear their hair, the way we are told that our hair in its natural state isn't good enough. That I have never had my hair chemically straightened is a fact of which I am immensely proud. I like to imply this is because I was racially conscious at an early age, but actually, like so many things, I owe it to my dad. Having seen black friends of his lose large chunks of hair due to the harsh chemicals involved in the straightening process, he forbade me to straighten my hair until I was sixteen. And of course by sixteen I was just conscious enough to know better, so I never fell prey to the chemical straighteners. That said, I only ever wore it tied back, or saturated with so much gel it had no option but to hang down: a product of the eighties, I was determined to have a fringe like all the other girls in my class. The one style I would never have contemplated was an Afro. An Afro was social death, and though I was conscious, I wasn't stupid. And then at university, I plucked up the courage to shave the lot off, to make what I thought was the boldest of statements: this is me, world, take it or leave it, but you can't escape it. The results were amazing. I loved having a shaved head, I loved how bold it made me feel, how radical it made me look. The in-your-faceness of it all. And then something in me changed. Slowly, after years of shaving my hair, I started to miss it. I'd forgotten what my own hair felt like, and I wanted to remember. Shaving started to feel like a cop-out instead of radical. Surely wearing my hair 'natural' was even more of a statement? Wearing it natural and at length was showing the world that I loved my hair in its natural state. Until now, wearing an Afro is probably the most rootsy thing I've ever done. I can't speak Tigrinya, I can't cook *injera*, but I can at least grow a decent Afro. And I had naively assumed that when I came to Eritrea I'd get extra brownie points for not having succumbed to Western ideals and having my hair straightened. My first indication that natural Afro hair would not necessarily go down as well as I'd hoped was the children in the street who'd shouted at me in my first days here. But I'd assumed it was the whole package – Afro, Western clothes, speaking English, etc. – that had got them all excited. Apparently, it was the Afro after all.

'He wants to know why your hair is like that,' says Medhanie.

'Like what?' I ask, trying not to sound defensive, especially after the skirt thing.

'Why is it not "done"? He says you look like a bandit.'

'Please tell him that this is how I always wear my hair. I like it like this. Natural,' I say, pointedly, surprised by how annoyed I feel. Later I will probably find this funny – that the dress I hated but bought because I thought it was demure turns out not to be demure enough, that the Afro that I (and lots of other black adults) wear thinking it is an outward signifier of how in touch we are with our roots actually screams the opposite. But right now it makes me sad and angry in equal measure. Despite my best efforts, I have failed in one of the few things I was confident about for the trip – that I'd at least be able to dress the part, to blend in. Dressing for the occasion is something I do, if not quite for a living then certainly as a hobby. My interest in clothes, not to mention shoes and accessories, knows no bounds. I write a beauty column in a national newspaper magazine for goodness' sake. Fashion faux pas are not my style. I did my research before I came. I read up on what was and was not appropriate for a woman of my age to wear. I went out and bought an entirely new wardrobe (any excuse) of clothes that lived up to the 'not too short/tight/low cut' guidelines various people gave me. And now it seems that on one of the few occasions when it really does matter, I've well and truly blown it with regard to my appearance.

As I vow never to wear this sodding dress again, I realize that I am also angry, not with myself for having misjudged things on the clothing front, but with my father. This man gave me up for adoption when I was a few days old, I have come all this way to find him and now here he is criticizing the length of my skirt. How dare he? He simply doesn't have the right.

I also make a mental note to buy myself a new skirt as soon as I get back to London, the shorter the better.

16

The pattern over the course of the next few days goes like this: I wake up around seven and have a few hours to myself, during which I find a café and sit outside eating a pastry. Then I stroll back to the hotel, making sure I'm back by around eleven, by which time my brothers are there, ready to pick me up. We go over to the same house in Mai Tameni, now by bus rather than taxi, and there we join my father, my sister, Zerai, and whichever new relatives have shown up that day. There is much crying and wailing as said new relatives greet me, and generally ask if I remember them (the answer is of course always 'no', for which I always feel I must apologize). Then there is food, followed by coffee, yet more afternoon visitors, and, inevitably, more crying. I sit among it all, like the centre of a cyclone, getting more and more confused as I am introduced to an endless stream of aunts, uncles and cousins.

I am meeting lots of people, but I don't feel as if I am learning anything other than that I have an awful lot of relatives, each one of whom 'cannot believe that God has brought me back' to them. I am starting to get wearily frustrated, and I am sure it is showing as I greet each new relative with slightly less enthusiasm than the last.

It is faintly ridiculous: a large part of my job involves interviewing people, and yet here I seem unable to garner any more than the barest of details. I am having real difficulties remembering people's names – the combination of the sheer number of people I am introduced to and the fact the names are unfamiliar to me means they slip from my grasp almost as soon as I have heard them. As this seems to cause undue offence, I have taken the matter into my own hands and started carrying around a notebook. When I am introduced to someone significant – a cousin or an aunt, say, I ask them to write their name down on the pad, in English as well as Tigrinya. Those who can't write, of whom there are many, generally give the pad to Medhanie or Zemichael and make them do the honours. I then try to copy the Tigrinya, and write an aide-mémoire in my own semi-official shorthand (part real shorthand, part my messy writing) which no one else can read, but which allows me to write crucial information – such as 'father's best friend, twinkly eyes' – which means I have a much better chance of committing them to memory.

After a couple of days my head is still swimming with aunts, uncles and the like, but I feel much happier now I seem to be able to remember who people are, though something is very definitely still missing. Although I have met plenty of people and am beginning to be able to work out who is who, I still don't really know very much about anyone. In terms of my siblings, for example, there is much I don't know. Sure, now I at least know their names, and how many children they have, but beyond that I remain largely ignorant. Who, for example, is the funny one, the shy one? Who is the clever one? Where will I fit into all this? Even on everyday facts my knowledge is weak. I realize, for example, that although I know my sister has seven children, I have no idea how she spends her days. Is she happy? Is her life as hard as I imagine? In fact, I don't know anything but the bare essentials about anyone, not even the

English speakers. I may be able to say, 'I have met my family,' but beyond that I don't have any real sense of them. If someone asked me, 'What is your oldest brother like?' I still wouldn't really be able to answer.

I become determined to find out more information, emotional things as well as core facts – things I can take with me, things that won't fade like the feeling of sitting next to them might. Reverting to what I know best, I have written a list of questions so that I can move through them in an almost businesslike manner.

It is the third or fourth day since I have met my family, and my brothers and I are on our way to the house as usual. 'Today you will say goodbye to Asrat, Timnit and Stephanos,' announces Medhanie as we step on to a crowded minibus. By now I know the drill, so I just grab a seat and let one of the others deal with paying for the ticket (it's just easier that way).

'What? They are leaving today?' I ask, trying to hide my irritation at having only just been told such a crucial piece of information. It never occurred to me they wouldn't stay for the duration of my trip.

'Timnit has to get back to her children – she has left her eldest daughter to look after the others for many days now; Stephanos' military leave is nearly over so he must return to the front; and Father has to get back to his cattle,' says Medhanie, matter-of-factly. As soon as he's finished I feel bad for acting like such a spoilt child: I may be free to flit around at will, but they clearly are not. If those three are going, then I will focus on them today, and do no more than exchange pleasantries with any new people who show up at the house, I decide. I don't want to leave this place having met lots of relatives but got to know none of them.

As soon as I walk into the by now familiar courtyard, I spot Timnit. A rush of emotion comes over me and I realize how much I want her to stay. I have only just found her – she can't be going already. I run up to her, deciding to ignore everything that stands between us and greet her as I would my other sister, Lydia. I give her a huge bear hug, kiss her on each cheek, then grab her hands and jump up and down half singing her name with each jump: 'Timnit, Timnit, Timnit!'

She bursts out laughing at my girlie display, then when I have finished she starts to do small jumps herself and shyly sings, 'Hannah, Hannah, Hannah!'

We both fall about while the others in the courtyard look on with a mixture of what looks like fear ('Who is this crazy woman we have welcomed into our family, does she have no idea how an Eritrean should behave?') and amusement, much in the same way you would humour a child, while hoping they know when to stop. Timnit and I eventually let each other go, and I am led into the sitting room. Timnit stays outside and goes back to whatever it was she was doing. I say hello to the room, and as yet again there are people in here I haven't met, I head over to my father and greet him. Once I sit down, I can see Timnit through the door. She is crouched down outside in front of a wooden board, chopping meat but looking into the room as if she'd rather be with us. Just looking at her and thinking of her leaving today stirs something inside. I am not ready for her to leave. I have not had enough of Timnit yet. I stand up and mutter something about going outside to help. Everyone looks slightly bemused. 'Where are you going?' asks Medhanie.

'I am going outside to help Timnit,' I reply, as if it's the most normal thing in the world for me to volunteer to help skin a goat, or whatever it is she's doing.

'No. You are not like the other women, you do not need to help cook,' he replies, motioning me to sit back down.

'I want to help,' I say, trying not to sound agitated that once again I am being told what to do by someone I have only just met; besides, for all he knows I could be a dab hand with a meat cleaver. He jumps up as if to follow me. 'It's fine, you stay where you are,' I say.

'But how will you speak to each other?' says Medhanie, sounding a little put out that his translation skills are not required. But I have had enough of interpretation. I want to spend some time with my sister, just the two of us. I want to see how we do at communicating on our own terms, instead of always through our brothers as interpreters. I think this is why I feel as if I haven't got to know anyone yet – it's impossible to get a handle on anyone when you are reliant on someone else to interpret their words. And far from making things easier, having your own words translated is a barrier to getting to know someone.

Outside, Timnit looks pleased to see me. I crouch down next to her and make elaborate 'I want to help cook' gestures. She understands me straight away, bounces up, heads into the kitchen and comes back with a low stool. I watch her chop and she chatters away to me in Tigrinya. It doesn't seem to matter that I have no idea what she is saying, she is happy to be talking to me and I am happy to be sitting here, listening to her. I imagine that she is telling me how to prepare the meat, or perhaps something about the best way to stop the knife slipping – nothing major, just some typically sisterly advice.

Timnit was around fourteen years old and already married when I was born. Although my father remarried soon after, as the eldest daughter Timnit would have had to look after the other children after our mother died. And as the eldest surely she will have remembered our mother the most and felt her sudden absence the keenest. I want to ask her how things were for her when our mother died, what she remembers about our mother, and what her life is like now. Others have told me that Timnit looks the most like our mother, so she must also be the best guide I have as to what I will look like when I am older. She is my older sister, but there are thirteen or fourteen years between us, so give or take a year or two, she could be my mother.

When you have spent your entire life looking for clues as to how you will age in the faces of strangers it is overwhelming to suddenly be looking into the face of your older sister. We have the same face shape, but hers is much, much thinner. Her eyes are huge, as is her smile, despite the fact she is missing quite a few teeth. Her skin is several shades darker than mine, and I feel pale, sickly almost, by comparison. In fact, my paleness has been commented on several times since I have met my family. I found it refreshingly ironic at first – no one has ever called me pale back home – but now it is beginning to grate: the fact I am lighter than everyone is yet another way in which I don't fit in, somehow a criticism of something which is not my fault, but which is taken as a signifier of my difference. I feel like saying, 'Well of course I'm paler than everyone else, but it's not my fault; I didn't choose to grow up under English clouds – in fact I had no say in the matter at all.'

Although you can tell easily that Timnit and I are sisters, it is even more obvious we have not had the same life. Even if you swapped our clothes – put me in her traditional Eritrean floor-length white dress, with a white pure cotton scarf covering my head and shoulders, and put Timnit in my 'too short' linen dress and swapped her braids for my Afro – any fool would be able to tell who had had the harder life.

Growing up in the Eritrean countryside cannot be easy. For the thirty years that I was growing up elsewhere, war, crop failures and lack of water were a part of Timnit's life. In the countryside, female genital cutting is the norm, marriages are arranged, and while the bride is anything from fourteen upwards, the groom is usually in his mid to late twenties. Even just the bare bones of my sister Timnit's life – married at fourteen, first child at seventeen, illiterate, trying to eke a living out of the land, dependent on foreign food aid to feed her seven children – are those of a typical Eritrean woman in the countryside. On top of all this, Timnit lost her mother at fourteen, her younger sister was killed during the war a few years later, and I, of course, was never around.

I want Timnit to absolve me somehow for taking her mother away from her: I want her to tell me, 'It's OK,' and that my being born didn't have the devastating effect upon her life I feel it must have had. I want all of my family to do it, but I need to hear it from Timnit the most – perhaps because with her mother dying, her sister dying and me being whisked off, it somehow feels as if she has lost the most – not just a mother and two sisters, but at such a young age having to be the woman of the family.

'How are you?' says a young female in clear, crisp English. I look up and see a young woman, in her late teens or early twenties, dressed in Western-style jeans and a red blouse.

'Hi. I'm very well – who are you?'

'I live here; it is wonderful to meet you.'

'Are you a relative too?' I ask, hoping she will stick around – it would be nice to see how a woman translates.

'My name is Nebiat, I am not a cousin, but you can call me your cousin,' says the woman, before turning to Timnit and saying something. They have a brief but animated chat and Timnit gets up, goes back to the kitchen and comes back with another stool. 'Timnit wants me to speak for her. She has some things she would like to say to you,' says Nebiat.

I smile: my enthusiasm for translating has suddenly returned, maybe because this time it is a woman, and someone who isn't as close as our brothers.

Timnit starts to speak. She is speaking so quickly that even Nebiat is having trouble keeping up. 'She says she has missed you every day since you were taken away,' says Nebiat, waving at Timnit to slow down. 'She says she lost two sisters, but now she has one back again. She wishes she did not have to leave, but she must, her children need her. She was supposed to leave yesterday, but she had not seen enough of you, she was not ready to leave. But today she must go, she is very sorry, but now you have seen each other, you will never be as far away from each other again, she has a sister back.' Timnit starts speaking again and then stops abruptly and goes into one of the rooms off the courtyard.

'Where is she going?' I ask Nebiat.

'She wants to give you something.'

'Oh no. Tell her she is not to give me anything, I have everything I need – I have met her and that is enough,' I plead, already embarrassed at my own oversight – why didn't I think to bring her anything? Timnit returns with what looks like a huge bag of grain and sets it down in front of us with a flourish.

'What is it?' I ask Nebiat.

'It's a sort of snack, but it brings good luck, because if you have it you will never go hungry,' says Nebiat.

'Please tell her I cannot take it,' I say.

'But you must, she will be very hurt if you do not accept it.'

'But I don't know what to do with it, and I will never be able to take it home.'

'Just take it and thank her. Later, when she is gone, you can give it to one of your brothers, or even the people in your hotel, as a gift, but you must let her give it to you,' says Nebiat, kindly, in soft tones so Timnit doesn't pick up the nature of what she is saying.

I turn to Timnit, '*Yekanyeley*,' I say, shakily.

'*Yekanyeley*!' she responds, seemingly thrilled at my attempt at thanking her in Tigrinya.

Then she motions for me to go back into the sitting room so she can get on with preparing the meal. I take the bag of grain with me, and marvel at what just happened. Timnit, my sister, who is for a large part dependent on foreign food aid, has just given me a sack of grain.

As I walk into the room, I remember the other day when I mistook my uncle for my father. I can't believe how long ago that seems. I go up to Asrat, my father, and we kiss, as usual, but with much less fanfare than on previous days. Things seem to have calmed down a lot emotionally, for which I am grateful. I am just about to attempt a couple of lines of Tigrinya, which I have learnt overnight, when he beats me to it: 'How are you?' he says. I do a double take. 'Howareyou?' he repeats in flawless English, rolling the three words into one.

I stand there speechless. My father has greeted me in my own language. He is a seventy-something illiterate farmer, and he has taken the trouble to learn a few words of English just so he can greet me in my own language. I am so overwhelmed with pride in him that it takes me a while to recover. 'I am very, very well,' I say, smiling the biggest smile I can. 'How are you?' I ask him back, slowly.

'Fine. Very fine,' he says proudly, his voice sounding even more statesmanlike in English than it does in Tigrinya.

A couple of hours later we have eaten, and now the moment I have been dreading has come. It is time for me to say goodbye to my father, my sister and my older brother. They are all leaving at first light, so we are to say goodbye now. The lovely Timnit has already said that if I were to come to the bus station with her she would not be able to board her bus. I don't feel I have spent enough time with Stephanos. At first I thought he was hiding from me – he looked like a rabbit trapped in headlights every time I went near him – but then Zemichael told me cities make him uncomfortable, since when he is not on the front he is with his wife and children in the same village as my father. He may be the one who looks the most like me, but he is also the only brother who doesn't speak English, and whose life is most different to my own. With Timnit I can attempt to bond in a girlie way. With Zemichael and Medhanie it's relatively easy because we can speak directly to each other; plus they are both professionals – a teacher and a statistician – albeit in a country blighted by war and hunger. But where does that leave Stephanos, apart from relying on his younger brothers so he can talk to his sister? His sister who cannot comprehend what his life is like, any more than I suppose he can comprehend hers. He has been a soldier for over twenty years. We don't speak the same language. Where is our common ground?

And yet, as with Timnit, faced with his departure I don't feel ready for it. Since I was told he was leaving today I have started to feel protective towards him. He is going back to the front, the border where just thirty miles separate him from Ethiopian troops, with the UN playing referee in between. What if the border flares up again like it did a couple of years ago? Something could easily happen to him. This could be the last time I see him, and even though we have barely spoken to each other, we have communicated, in our own way. I don't think the shock and overwhelming sense of emotion I felt when I first saw him will ever abate. It was like standing in front of a male version of myself. His skin was darker, his cheekbones more pronounced, but there was no escaping the fact this man was my older brother. For those first few days, when it seemed that he was keeping a distance, I wasn't sure if he'd felt it like I had. But then one early evening he and the other two were walking me back to my hotel, down the main street, and Stephanos and Zemichael disappeared into a shop. When Stephanos came out a few moments later, his tiny (Hannah-sized) hands were holding what looked like a text-book. 'He wants to be able to speak to you,' said Zemichael, by way of explanation. 'He is going to try to teach himself English while he is on the front.'

That was the moment I knew Stephanos knew what I was feeling.

As he prepares to go, I want to tell him to be careful, to look after himself, that I will be reading any news about the Eritrean–Ethiopian border thinking of him – but don't feel like I can without sounding patronizing. After all, he has been a soldier for the majority of his life and nearly all of mine and I can't just show up now and start telling him to be careful. With most of the country on national service, it doesn't do to dwell on how dangerous war is. So I guess I'll just do what everyone else seems to be doing and not make a big fuss. If my father can say goodbye to Stephanos without getting emotional, I must do the same. So I kiss him three times, tell him that when I am at home trying to learn Tigrinya, I will be thinking of him on the front trying to learn English, that we will do it together. He laughs, smiles and nods in agreement, and says something to Zemichael: 'He says you are younger, so you must learn more Tigrinya.' I laugh in agreement, enjoying the fact that for once I don't mind someone telling me to learn the language.

And then I turn to my father. I don't know why but saying my goodbyes in the reverse order that I said the hellos just seemed right. My sister, my brother, and then my father. Before today, his was the only goodbye that had been troubling me. I had been dreading it almost from the moment we met. I knew it wasn't going to be easy, no matter now well I got to know him, or whether or not we 'bonded'. My father represents everything, my whole story. He is the only one who can tell me everything about my adoption. It was his decision alone. And the moment he made that decision he changed the course of my life. I knew that as soon as he left, I would feel bereft in some way, as if the main piece of the jigsaw was missing. As soon as I knew he was alive, nearly ten years ago, I obsessed about my father dying before I plucked up the courage to meet him. Meeting him has only heightened the fear – now I will know exactly what I am missing. Watching him prepare to leave feels like watching myself get mugged or burgled. I know I will get over it, but I'd rather not have to. In my head he was the big prize of this trip, my siblings the bonus.

It is difficult to describe the feeling of going from thinking you are an orphan to being told you have a living birth parent. It doesn't just shift the world's view of you, it shifts your entire view of yourself. Suddenly you have a root. A family tree. Something from which you came, and grew. It – your history, your life – no longer just begins and ends with you. You now go back, beyond your years, and there is living, breathing proof of it. With adoption comes a lifetime of wondering if you did something wrong, if it was your fault in some way. And the only people who can answer that question are the people who gave you up. So no matter how many siblings or half-siblings an adoptee learns they have, if they do decide to trace it is always their birth parents they are most desperate to meet.

I am deeply aggrieved at my father for leaving so soon. I know he has to go, I know that he has a herd of cattle to look after, not to mention six other children, but the little girl in me wants to shout that it is not fair. They have had him all their lives, surely it's my turn? He must know I have lots to ask him – or perhaps that is why he is leaving? Is he doing a runner before things get too tricky, while we're still on small talk?

'He says he must go now,' says Medhanie, interrupting my thoughts.

'Yes, I know,' I reply, trying not to snap like a spoilt child, but not managing to stop the slight wobble in my voice.

'He wants to tell you that he is a very old man. You must come back and visit him quickly.'

Great, I think, even he thinks he's about to die. My eyes start to well up.

'He says not to be sad. He is not sad, because now you have met your family you will never be as far apart again.' My father kisses me again, and says some more words, but no one translates them – they don't need to: by now I know he is thanking God for reuniting his family. By the time I wake up the next morning, all three of them will be on their way home, my father and my sister to their villages and my brother back to the front. The journey will take each of them at least two days.

17

Now my father and Timnit have left I feel differently about being here. Things that haven't bothered me before have started to do my head in. I have been seriously contemplating moving my flight forward, making up some sort of emergency that I have to return home for. For the first time in my life, I am homesick. I have never understood homesickness. If anything, I always saw it as a sign of weakness. But now I am desperate to get back to my flat, my friends, my life. I am sick of being taken to the house in Mai Tameni every morning to meet yet more relatives. Without my father and sister these visits to the house have lost their purpose, their warmth. Now I just show up to be prodded, poked and cooed over by distant aunts and uncles. I have lost my sense of self – I no longer feel like a person or like I'm on a personal journey, but like I'm a travelling side show, or a prize cow. I find it hard not to snarl when asked, for the umpteenth time, 'Why don't you speak Tigrinya?' If one more person tells me it is my mother tongue I am liable to shout back, 'My mother is dead!' such is the strength of my feeling.

Things I found interesting, even I am ashamed to say a bit exciting, when I first arrived have started to get me down – the relentless heat, the children selling cigarettes on the street, the constant presence of soldiers. I saw all those things before, but I don't think I ever related them to my family. This is my family's reality, something they see every day, and as such it no longer seems quite so exciting. I've had enough. I want to walk down the street without feeling like such an outsider, a tourist. When I first got here I was so overwhelmed by the fact everyone looked like me I didn't notice the subtle differences. Now I see how people look at me when I pass them. I might look Eritrean, but I don't look local. I am a 'returnee'. There are plenty of us around, especially in the summer months, and we stand out no matter how much we try to kid ourselves otherwise: our clothes, our hairstyles, our shoes, even the shade of our skin marks us out as 'not from around here'. The lucky among us can speak the language, but even then our accents give us away. We acknowledge each other on the street, and strike up conversations in cafés – it's a relief, you see, to be speaking in English, or German, or Swedish, anything so long as it's not Tigrinya. There's even a hierarchy among us. The English-speaking returnees (Americans, Canadians, British) are a bit sniffy towards the other European ones (largely Swedish or German), seemingly slightly embarrassed by them. And yet, because of the large number of Swedish and German Eritreans, many of the bigger hotels and restaurants have menus in those languages rather than in English, which pisses the English-only speakers right off. To make international relations worse, most of the continental European returnees can speak Tigrinya, where many of the others don't, which makes the non-Tigrinya speakers among us a mite defensive.

The returnees from Arab countries have an easier time of things since Arabic is Eritrea's second working language, so they can usually get by language-wise. And then there are those from Ethiopia, who speak a combination of Amharic, English and Tigrinya, depending on how old they were when they left Ethiopia. They can get along with pretty much everyone, so in some sense they are top of the tree, despite the fact many of them were kicked out of Ethiopia during the last border war in 2000, so haven't come here through choice.

Seeking out other returnees becomes something of a guilty pleasure. As does checking my e-mail daily, and even the odd call home. One evening I meet up with some of these new friends. Eli, the daughter of a friend of my cousin's, lives in New York, and Jonas, a friend of hers from her school days, lives in Camden, London. The three of us go to an Italian restaurant and eat lasagne and drink red wine. If I closed my eyes I could be at home. Later we go to a club run by a friend of theirs, another returnee, but one who has decided to do more than just visit and is trying to make a go of things here. The bar is playing up to date R & B and hip hop, and we drink vodka cocktails and dance all evening. It could be a typical London night out, and we all seem equally desperate for it. The only thing that spoils the illusion is the fact the only other people in the bar are either returnees like us or UN soldiers with prostitutes.

The next morning, my head is banging and I realize I had barely drunk any alcohol for nearly two weeks until last night. I have developed a bit of a taste for Asmara beer, but as I'm not usually a beer drinker and (I suspect more crucially) as it's not really on for women to drink in public, I've been sticking with soft drinks, apart from the incident with the ouzo when I first met my family. But last night we were drinking spirits and even though I'm suffering, I'm getting a bit of a kick from the familiar feeling of a hangover. In fact, headache aside, I feel much better. It's as if my London-style evening out has rejuvenated me, given me back some of my confidence and sense of self, and now I feel as if I could happily stay here for a little longer. Can I be homesick and want to stay longer at the same time? When I arrived, before I met my family, I loved it here, and wished I'd booked a longer visit. Then, a week or so later I was so exhausted by the place that I was contemplating going home early. But I can't stop thinking about my father and sister now that they have gone back to the villages – how will I ever get to know them or anyone else here if I can only see them for a couple of days?

When we said goodbye that was supposed to be it, for this trip at least. But as soon as my father and Timnit left I started to feel low. Without them in front of me I realized how little I know about them, about their lives. What kind of a daughter doesn't know what her father's house looks like? What kind of a sister has never met her nieces and nephews? Sure, I've met my father and my sister, touched them, taken a few photographs, but as soon as they left, what little I have learned has turned to dust. I have trouble remembering details. It's as if they've died: one minute they were standing in front of me, the next they were gone and I can't remember what their voices were like. I have tried thinking of other things, hooking up with some of the friends I've made, going back into holiday mode, hoping memories of my father and sister would rise gently to the surface, but nothing has worked – anything I do to distract myself just makes me feel even further away from them.

I should be feeling satisfied, fulfilled in some way, but instead I am agitated, as if someone has fed me a delicious morsel, then denied me the main course. My father, sister and brother have been dangled in front of me just long enough for me to get a taste for them, and then they've been whisked away. I need another hit.

18

I decide to call Medhanie and tell him I want to go to the villages.

'Which villages?' he asks.

'My father's village, Timnit's village, the village Himan was buried in, and the village where I was born,' I reply, aware that it is probably an impractical request, but trying to make it sound otherwise.

'Why do you want to go? You have met everyone, the villages are very far away, and life there is not easy. You will be very shocked. I do not think you should go, not yet. You are not ready,' says Medhanie, in a voice that is both stern and protective.

'What do you mean, not yet?' I ask. I have an inkling what he is getting at, but I need to be sure.

'You know nothing about village life,' says Medhanie bluntly. 'You will find the things you see too difficult. You will get upset. It will be too hard for you. You are not strong enough. Go to the villages another time – go in the rainy season when there is some green. Things are a little better then. Do not go now.'

I am stunned. I had expected some practical resistance to my request – time factors mostly, as going to the villages would mean I wouldn't be around to meet any more aunts and uncles – but I hadn't ever expected to be told I shouldn't go, that I wouldn't be able to cope.

'Let's meet up later and talk about it,' I say, trying to diffuse the situation. Besides, I'll have a better chance of putting my case across in person, once I've planned a slightly more sophisticated argument than 'But I want to go'.

Medhanie and I meet that evening and have an impassioned conversation – him re-emphasizing how hard life in the villages is, adding a few more basics designed to put me off: 'There is no running water, no electricity, no toilets,' and me resorting to emotional blackmail, telling Medhanie how much seeing where my father and sister live would mean to me, how long I have waited for this, how far I have come, and so on. Eventually he says: 'Do you have a helicopter?'

'A helicopter? No, but I could probably hire one,' I reply. I have no idea if this is the case, and given I have problems hailing a taxi in this country my chances of managing to find and hire a helicopter, complete with pilot, are slim, but now is not the time for negativity.

'That won't be necessary – I was joking,' he chortles. 'Yes, OK, we can go to the villages.'

'Oh, I'm sorry.' I try to sound amused, but just feel bad I didn't get his joke, as if I've let him down in some way, or missed a chance at sharing something special.

'Do you have a four-wheel drive?' he asks, after an awkward silence.

I tell him I don't.

'Well, that is OK – as long as you have your driving licence with you it will be very easy and not too expensive to hire a car,' he says.

'Ah – I don't have a licence. I can't drive,' I confess.

'You can't drive?' his voice lifts and he is smiling again. 'You can't drive? But everyone who comes here from outside can drive,' he says, more as a question than a statement.

'Well, not me,' I reply.

'Well, neither can I. Ha! That is fantastic, we will learn together,' declares Medhanie gleefully, and I wonder if he realizes what a sweet thing he has just said. There are a few seconds of silence, and then he gets back to the matter at hand. 'There is not enough time to go to all four villages by bus, it is not possible in one trip. Our father's village is very far from Timnit's and Himan's is very far from all of them. If you go to Himan's you cannot go to the others. But we can go to our father's village, then come back to Asmara so you can rest for a couple of days, and then go to Timnit's. If we have time, we can reach the village we were born in from Timnit's. How does that sound?' he asks.

'That sounds fine. Thank you.'

My father's village is the furthest away, so the plan is to go there first, via Keren, where we will stay overnight at Zemichael's house. Zemichael, who is coming with us, is thrilled about the new plan as it means he will be able to introduce me to his wife and son.

Predictably, I have a hangover when we set off, as a result of another night out with the other returnees. Perhaps it's the effect of suddenly having older siblings fuss over me, or the hassle of travelling in a country where I don't speak the language, but I have definitely regressed, and the hangover makes me feel even more like a sullen teenager. Although it goes against the grain, it is becoming easier to let everyone else make the decisions and for me to go along with them, than to get annoyed, when what they've decided is what will happen anyway. I had no idea we were going to Keren before it was announced yesterday evening, by which time I had already arranged to go out with Eli and Jonas. As a result, my head is banging and I am thankful that even though it is only 7 a.m. it is bright enough to warrant wearing sunglasses. The bus station is manic with travellers and hawkers alike. Boys in their teens run up and down waving tickets and shouting the destination of their bus, while the driver sits in the nearest café waiting for the bus to fill up. Women carry children in one arm, live chickens in the other. Yet more young boys load bags on top of the buses. Girls walk around selling nuts, twigs which look like liquorice but which I later learn are for cleaning your teeth, and fresh limes, for travel sickness. I buy a lime in the hope it will do the trick for alcohol-induced nausea.

'Kerenkerenkerenkerenkeren!' shouts a boy of about fourteen. He says it so quickly it sounds as if he's spraying bullets from a toy gun.

'That's the Keren bus,' says Zemichael. 'Give me your bags and I will get us a seat. You should go to the toilet now while you can.'

'How long is the journey?' I ask, hopefully.

'Well, it depends. The journey can be done in about three hours, but first we have to wait for the bus to fill up.' Obediently I head for the toilet and when I return find it is still pretty much just my two brothers and me on the bus. We sit there for over an hour, but hardly anyone boards our bus. Were it not for the fact that I was dreading the bus journey in the first place due to my hangover I'd be getting agitated by now, but as it is I am happy to just sit and wait, sniffing my lime. Zemichael evidently is not. He gets up and announces he is going to find the driver. Half an hour later, he comes back without the driver, but with a different, younger boy. Some shouting ensues between the two bus boys, and the younger one, despite his age, is obviously triumphant, as he transfers our not inconsiderably heavy bags from the roof of the big bus to a much smaller yellow minibus. Zemichael explains to me that our new bus is smaller, and we shouldn't have to wait so long for it to fill up. An hour and a half later, our minibus is full to bursting, and we finally head off.

I have always thought of Keren as the place I was born. Even when I knew virtually nothing about Eritrea, I knew I was from Keren. Years ago, when I applied for my first passport, I wrote Keren under 'Place of birth'. I should probably have written Eritrea – I doubt the passport officials wanted quite so much detail – but I wanted to write Keren. It made me feel as if I knew more about my background than I did. As the bus leaves Asmara it becomes apparent how little I have seen of Eritrea. I arrived at night, which meant I missed out on seeing the land mass from above, and I have spent all my time in the capital, and most of that has been confined to one house. Thanks to the endless stream of relatives, I may feel as if I have met the entire population, but I have hardly seen the country. After just thirty minutes the landscape changes significantly. The dusty, bumpy road is replaced by smooth tarmac, and the bustling city by a landscape as dramatic and mountainous as it is dry and arid. So this is what they mean by scorched earth. The land looks lunar, all red and cracked, with few trees and dry rivers. Every so often we pass a cluster of tiny oblong concrete houses, always single-storey, usually painted white with corrugated-iron roofs. I can tell without looking inside that most of them have little more than one, perhaps two rooms. The only things on the road are buses, the pristine white UN four-wheel drives and the occasional truck, which leaves behind it such a thick cloud of exhaust that everyone automatically closes their windows as soon as they see one on the horizon – everyone apart from me, of course, who never remembers and gets shouted at by the other passengers. We pass more burnt-out tanks than we do people. And camels. And goats. At first I take a picture of each one, much to the amusement of my fellow passengers, to whom it's probably akin to a London tourist taking a picture of a red bus, but after three hours of the things, even I become a bit blasé about them. But the countryside holds my attention for the duration of the trip. Keren means 'mountain' in Tigrinya. The lime has worked as despite the twists, turns and incredibly steep inclines, my nausea has gone, my ears are popping and I can't get enough of the view. All around me, the only things I can see are the mountains. They are below us, they are above us, they are rolling back all the way to the horizon no matter in which direction I look. A wave of heat gives those furthest away a misty film-set quality, as if only the ones immediately in front of us are real, and those further back are painted on to a screen.

I have been warned by Zemichael that Keren is hotter, drier and far dustier than Asmara, because it is in the highlands. But he also assures me I will love it just as much, if not more. I don't tell him, but I am already fond of it in my own way. The word Keren has always been in my passport, but I have never seen it. And now I will. Better still, Zemichael has just told me Keren is Eritrea's third city – after Asmara and Massawa – just as the Manchester I grew up in technically comes after London and Birmingham. I decide this can only be a good omen, of which there haven't been nearly enough lately.

19

The smooth tarmac gives way to a bumpy, dusty track, which lets me know we have arrived. There is about an hour to go before sunset. 'My dad told me to watch the sunset from the roof of the Keren Hotel,' I say to my brothers.

'He has been here?' asks Zemichael.

'Yes, I told you, he's been here lots.' This is another problem with constant translation. Even though you tell people things several times, I suspect less than half of it actually goes in. I have told my brothers that my dad has been to Eritrea numerous times. I have told them that he is an expert, that he has written books on the region, but somehow it doesn't seem to sink in. I am about two explanations away from saying, 'Don't you know who he is?' And yet when I told some of the friends of my cousin Gaim's in Asmara who my dad was, they all got very excited and started to introduce me as David Pool's daughter. This is the kind of thing that would obviously crucify my image at home, and yet here I love it, love being thought of as David Pool's daughter. One man even said the words, '*The* David Pool? The great friend of Eritrea?' I can't wait to get back and tell my dad.

We get off the bus and decide to go straight to the Keren Hotel, so as to ensure we catch the sunset. Medhanie and I order two Asmara beers, teetotal Zemichael orders a Sprite, and we pull our chairs round so we all face the horizon. From the roof of the hotel you can see where Keren finishes and the countryside begins. Weirdly, it reminds me of Las Vegas – a city that has randomly sprung up in the middle of a desert. Without thinking, I tell my brothers this.

'What is Las Vegas?' asks Zemichael.

'It's a city in the desert in America. It's horrid really, full of casinos and fat Americans,' I reply, remembering a comment Medhanie made about how amazed he was that Americans managed to get so big.

'So you have been to America?' asks Zemichael.

'Yes.'

'Where else?' he asks, and I instantly wish I'd kept my stupid thoughts about Vegas to myself.

'Chicago, New York and Los Angeles,' I say, hoping that will suffice.

'No, where else in the world have you been?' asks Zemichael, ever the pedantic teacher.

By this point I am feeling uncomfortable. I am their younger sister, they are supposed to be the worldly ones. And until this moment that has been the order of things since we met. They have taken care of me, bought my bus tickets, translated for me, generally looked out for me, and now I feel as if I'm about to blow their cover by making it painfully clear that not only have I seen more of the world than them, but I did it without them. 'Mostly Europe – you know, France, Germany, Switzerland, that kind of thing,' I say, trying to make foreign travel sound as mundane as possible.

'What about outside of Europe?' continues Zemichael, not picking up, or ignoring, how uncomfortable this is making me feel.

'Well, then it's just America, Sri Lanka and Australia,' I say, desperately trying not to sound smug.

'I have never left my country. It is impossible for me to leave: I would not get a visa,' says Zemichael, wistfully. 'Medhanie has at least been to Ethiopia. What kind of teacher has never left his country?'

I have yet to figure out Zemichael and Medhanie properly. I assumed I would bond most easily with them because their lives are the most easily comparable to my own. All three of us are young university-educated professionals living in a major city, and of course they both speak English. But if anything they have seemed the most emotionally elusive, the hardest to pin down. It is not something that is easy to put my finger on. Suffice to say that in the last couple of days in the house in Mai Tameni I'd find myself gravitating towards the traditionally dressed women, rather than, say, those in Western clothes. And it is the same with my brothers. We should have the most in common, but that makes things harder not easier. It is precisely because our lives are comparable that the differences between them seem so great.

Medhanie, for example, is a statistician for the government. He is single, earns a good wage, and yet, because of property shortages in Asmara, he shares a small room with three other colleagues. I, on the other hand, have just bought my own one-bedroom flat in central London. I take at least three foreign holidays per year; my brothers are not able to leave their country. I go into a state of panic if I gain a few pounds in weight; they worry whether their older sister will have enough to feed her family. I feel proud of myself if I manage to take clothes I no longer want to my local charity shop; they give as much of their earnings as they can afford to our father. I think it faintly glamorous to see the UN on the streets; they are desperate for them to leave, but know the moment they do the border with Ethiopia will become unstable and they could be called up to guard it. Every time I think we have found some common ground, it is tinged with a cruel irony. For example, I lived it up for three years while at Liverpool University; Medhanie went to university in Addis Ababa, only to spend eight months in a prison cell, along with fellow Eritrean classmates, accused of spying by the Ethiopian government. The list goes on, and all it seems to do is highlight how very different we are. I always come out of it looking like the lucky one, the one who got away. There will be an awkward silence while we all realize that fact, and I'll want to say, 'Yes, but it wasn't my choice; I would rather have not been adopted,' but I can't think of a way of saying it that doesn't make me sound even more conceited.

But I think Zemichael gets it. There have been a couple of times when he has shown me he understands. Like when Medhanie told me how lucky I was to have been put in the orphanage as it meant I was adopted by 'the white couple'. I was so shell-shocked by what I saw as his insensitivity that I didn't know how to respond. Zemichael stepped in and said, 'But Medhanie, you are the luckiest of us all: you had our father, you had a normal childhood.' And he is always quick to jump to my defence when someone is admonishing me for not speaking Tigrinya.

Zemichael knows how hard it is to try and come into a new family, into this family, because he had to do it. When he was seven or eight, Zemichael was sent to live in Dekemhare, a former industrial town about half an hour's drive from Asmara. The exact reason is unclear, but it seems my father's new wife was overwhelmed by the five children she had inherited, which is hardly surprising given she was only around fifteen years old herself. As Zemichael was the youngest, and therefore the most demanding of attention, it was deemed easier to send him away. Some describe the place he was sent to as a boarding school, others as a children's home. It doesn't really matter what you call it, because either way, no one visited him for years, so to all intents and purposes he grew up without his family.

The children's home was hard. There were about a hundred and forty children, and it was run by strict Protestants, which Zemichael understandably became too. This immediately marks him out as an oddball in the family, as they are all Orthodox Christians. On turning eighteen Zemichael left Dekemhare and did the three- or four-day journey to his father's village in the north. When we met, Zemichael said two things which endeared him to me: 'Now I am no longer the only stranger in the family,' swiftly followed by, 'Your hands and feet are as small as mine.'

Zemichael didn't just find his family – he also found mine for me. When he left Dekemhare, one of his first stops was the orphanage in Asmara that someone had told him his sister had been put in. It is Zemichael who wrote the letter that found its way to my dad, the letter that first told us I wasn't an orphan, that I had a family in Eritrea. Without Zemichael making that first move, without his detective work or his determination to be reunited with his family, his entire family, I wouldn't be sitting here having a drink with my brothers.

Every so often I get twinges of jealousy from him, and yet never once has he said, 'Why were you adopted and me not?' If anything he is the one that gets it the most: he knows that no matter how easy my life seems compared to theirs, I'd much rather have grown up here, with my family, with them.

'Look at the sunset, do you see it like that in London?' asks Medhanie, breaking the silence.

'No,' I laugh, 'in London you can barely see the sky.'

The sunset turns the whole sky a burnt orange, casting a warm glow over the buildings in its shadow. As soon as it disappears into the horizon, my brothers stand up, as if the show is over, and we get ready to leave. We walk down the stairs, through the hotel and outside into the street, which is much fuller than when we arrived, and I immediately notice the big difference, other than the heat and the dust, between Keren and Asmara. Asmara, with its chic art deco surroundings, is like a grown up compared to Keren, where the style and colour come not from the architecture but from the people. Unlike Asmara, where a good proportion of people are in Western clothes, in Keren they wear traditional dress – the brightly coloured dresses of the Bilen women, or the white jellabas of the Tigre men. Though quite obviously the poorer cousin in terms of the money coming into the city (quality of the roads, number of shops, etc.), in terms of its people Keren is much richer. The result is that while Asmara has a distinctly European feel, Keren is unmistakably African. The markets are more vibrant, the people even more relaxed, as if they have nothing to prove – I can't help but compare it to Manchester.

As we walk the dust track to where Zemichael lives with his wife and son, I can barely contain my excitement at all this colour. 'It is the people that make Keren beautiful, the people and the mountains,' says Zemichael, in response to my constant enthusing. Every few moments I think how wonderfully different I will feel whenever I see the word Keren in my own passport from now on. I will be able to picture the mountains and the colours, instead of having a black hole where an image should be. I will be able to describe the haze of sunset and the smell of the market. I might even start adopting a wistful tone and a slight air of mystery as I look into the middle distance and say, 'Ah, Keren, it means mountain, you know. Beautiful place, beautiful people.' That'll put an end to those pitying looks I get when I give my usual response of, 'I don't know what it looks like: I left when I was a baby.'

20

As we walk through the centre of the city, Zemichael is stopped every few minutes by a friend or some sort of relative. It seems like every other person in Keren is related to us. By now I am used to the way a five-minute stroll can take for ever in this country, but this is different. It's like walking down the street with a minor celebrity. Unlike everyone else, when this happens Zemichael doesn't introduce me to each and every single person. Instead he picks and chooses, introducing me only to those to whom I am either related or he is close. This is such a relief, as I am now tiring so much of the constant introductions that the ritual, followed as it inevitably is by 'Why don't you speak Tigrinya?' is turning me into a sullen teenager.

'Everyone knows who you are,' I say to Zemichael.

'It is because I am a teacher. I have either taught them or I am teaching their children,' he explains.

'You must be very proud,' I say, realizing only as I say the words that that is how I am feeling about my brother.

'Would you like to see the school?' he asks, modestly ignoring my comment.

'I'd love to. Is this the school I would have gone to?'

'Yes. I didn't go there because I was sent to Dekemhare, but it is where Medhanie went,' says Zemichael, not bothering to hide the bitterness in his voice.

We cross the road and walk towards a large municipal

single-storey building, with once-white walls that are now red with dust. From the outside, the only thing that gives away the building's identity is a white sign that reads (in English) 'Keren School' in shaky black handwriting. Once inside the cool interior, it is so unmistakably a school that I instantly stand straight and feel like a naughty pupil for trespassing after hours. 'It's amazing – it feels like a school at home,' I say, as we walk along an empty corridor decorated with students' artwork.

'Come and see my classroom,' says Zemichael, visibly pleased with my reaction. He opens the door to an empty room that looks as if it would hold about thirty desks.

'It looks great,' I say, deciding not to comment on the lack of furniture. 'How many students do you have?'

'About sixty.'

'Gosh, that's an awful lot. In England people think anything over thirty is too many.'

'That's in the morning,' continues Zemichael, in a measured tone, 'and then another sixty in the afternoon.'

We walk outside and I see what constitutes the playground – an area about a quarter of the size of a football pitch, with a low wall around it. I think back to my Manchester comprehensive days. Even there we had numerous well-kept green fields, netball and tennis courts, and a hard concourse. And that's before I even start to think about the high-tech language lab, the fully equipped gymnasium and the science block that, granted, I didn't see much of. And we thought we were hard done by compared to the private schools. 'Are there any computers?' I ask, pretty sure of the answer but needing to make my own point. I don't want to make Zemichael feel any worse about his school's lack of facilities, but I do think he'd appreciate knowing just how different things are elsewhere, in the same way that he wanted to know where in the world I had travelled.

'Computers?' laughs Zemichael.

'Yes, in English schools there is usually at least one classroom full of computers.'

'No. There are no computers. What else do you have in your English schools?'

In an understated manner I tell him about the other things, saving the best until last: 'And some schools have panic buttons,' I say as nonchalantly as I can manage.

'What is a panic button?' he asks.

'It's a button under the teacher's desk so that if a student gets out of control, the teacher can push the button and the police will come.'

Zemichael and Medhanie both look suitably horrified.

We leave the school, and even though it is early evening, there are pupils milling around outside. A young girl who looks about twelve or thirteen years old rushes up to Zemichael and starts speaking. Zemichael gives her some of my bags that he has been carrying, and she walks down the street with us. 'She wants to practise her English with you,' he says, turning to me.

'Great,' I say. Then, to the girl, in my best BBC voice, 'What is your name?'

The girl looks at the floor and laughs shyly.

I try again, but despite what Zemichael said she's not having any of it. I suddenly feel too tired for this. Zemichael says a few words to her in Tigrinya. Whatever he said works (a threat of detention perhaps?) because when he's finished she has found her voice.

'Howareyou?' she says, turning the phrase into one word and rolling the 'r' in a way everyone seems to do here.

'I am fine. How are you?' I ask, and we walk down the street exchanging pleasantries, which makes me feel like I've done a good deed, except of course she is carrying nearly all my belongings on her head.

We turn off the main street and into a dusty lane, which seems to signify we are in the residential area, and say goodbye to the girl. I ask Zemichael if I should give her some money for carrying the bags but he says she would be hurt if we tried to. We walk a little further and then Zemichael stops in front of a high wall that is the same reddish white as everything else here. We step through a tall, thin metal gate in the wall into a small courtyard, with its obligatory chickens, and walk towards the small building on the left. A woman with a softly pretty face comes out to greet us and a toddler runs through her legs to be scooped up by Zemichael. Zemichael seems to grow several inches in height and has a smile so wide it is contagious. 'This is my wife, Senait,' he says, after he has kissed her.

'Hi. *Kemay alekee?*' I ask.

'I am fine,' says Senait, in English. 'Welcome.'

'And this,' says Zemichael, grandly, 'is my son, Jonathan.'

'Hello, Jonathan,' I say, as Zemichael hands me the baby. Jonathan takes one look at his new aunt and bursts out crying. Senait, who has been saying hello to Medhanie, comes to my rescue (or is she coming to Jonathan's?) and takes the baby back. Zemichael leads us into their house.

My brother and his wife are both teachers. Compared to the majority of Eritreans, they are well off – lower middle class at least. And yet they live in one room. Their family home is roughly the size of my small one-bedroom London flat. Their bed and Jonathan's cot are in one corner, a sofa suite and coffee table are along one wall, and a curtain divides off the kitchen area. There is no sink, fridge or any other things that would signify it as the kitchen, other than a tiny traditional stove and what looks like a washing-up bowl. There are lights on and I can hear the loud static of a television somewhere nearby, so there is definitely electricity, but I have no idea where they get their water. Despite this, the place is spotless. 'The toilet is next door; we share it with the other homes in the compound,' says Zemichael, seeing me trying to figure things out. 'Do you think our home is very small?' he asks.

'Not at all. My place is about the same size,' I say, pleased that for once I am not banging on about how big or flash something is.

'How many do you share with?' he asks.

'No one, just me,' I say, sensing I am about to be rumbled.

'Is it just one room?' he asks, suspiciously.

'Yes – well no, not really: there is a separate room for my bed, and my kitchen and bathroom are separate,' I say, for the first time very aware of how wasteful it sounds for one person to have all those rooms.

That evening Senait prepares *nai tsom* – a selection of vegetables with *injera*, usually eaten by the Orthodox during fasting times – for my benefit as my stomach has started to react badly to everything else. After dinner Zemichael gets out his photo album. The most recent pictures are of his wedding, Medhanie's graduation and other typical family occasions, but it's the pictures at the start that give the game away. Pictures of Zemichael's face staring out among a hundred other young boys. Pictures of him with all his belongings, such as they were, stuffed in his pocket. 'We carried everything we owned in our pockets so no one could steal them,' he says.

I ask him what it was like in the children's home.

'It was tough. They teach you to forget about your family. That's how you had to be. You become so reliant on yourself that you don't know how to be with other people, how to be with family,' he says.

I ask him why he was sent there. There is a long pause and I wonder if I have overstepped the mark. I know how it feels when people ask me the same – in my head it translates as, 'Why didn't your own family want you?'

'It's the one question I want to know the answer to but am too afraid to ask,' says Zemichael. 'If I ask my father now, I know that he will tell me that after our mother died it was very difficult. I was a small child and he couldn't look after me, he had to look after the cattle, his new wife was young and it's difficult being a stepmother. I know my father thought he was giving me a better life in the children's home, but it was very very hard.'

I ask him if the family visited.

'My father couldn't visit and neither could Stephanos because they were on the front, but Medhanie used to visit. Even when he was a student and had no money he would try and send me as many nakfa as he could, and in the children's home a few nakfa went a long way. I'd boast about him, say "Look, this is my brother" – I'd be so proud of him when he visited. At the home you don't know how to be close to people. All you know is how to queue up for food, go to bed at a certain time, go to sleep when the light is turned off for you. When you leave at eighteen it is hard. So many of my brothers and sisters from the home have died or ended up begging. They can't cope when they leave: they only know how to live inside the home. The one good thing the orphanage gave me is God. And it taught me forgiveness. And that's why when I came out I went in search of my family. But that also was not easy. When I found them I was always the odd one out. We have so many aunts and uncles and relatives that I don't know. Timnit, Stephanos and Medhanie know everyone, and I am always the odd one out. Sometimes I feel like a stranger. But now I am no longer the strangest, or the youngest – now that's you,' says Zemichael. He's laughing, but the gentleness of his voice lets me know he has never spoken like that to anyone before, at least not to anyone in the family.

Zemichael then turns to the next page of the photo album, and there it is, the picture that started the whole ball rolling, the picture my dad left with the orphanage when he visited on impulse ten years ago.

21

It is getting late, and we have to be up early as the journey to our father's village will take anything from a few hours to a full day, depending on how lucky we get with buses. We go to bed and then get up again at four in the morning to give ourselves a chance of travelling before it gets too hot. I get dressed as quietly as I can so as not to wake Senait or Jonathan. Having been warned the villages are super-conservative, I have brought the longest skirt I packed with me – a floor-length denim tent-like number. I put on the skirt and a long-sleeved white shirt. The only part of this outfit I like is the flowers on the shirt. On the advice of my brothers, I also put on a headscarf, to cover up my offending Afro. We silently drink tea, eat some bread, and then tiptoe out of the compound. Medhanie and Zemichael, true to previous form, won't let me carry anything heavy. When I first met them I found it charming that my brothers kept asking to carry my bags. Then, after just a couple of days, I started to find it irritating beyond belief. I hated having to ask for my purse, or my room key or my water every five minutes. I felt stripped of what little power I have here. But over the past couple of weeks I have learnt to pick my battles carefully, and while I would usually object to not being allowed to carry anything, it is four in the morning and the principles of equality are far from my mind. Instead, I make myself useful by carrying the torch and making sure it lights Zemichael's path, since he is the one leading us through the otherwise unlit streets.

To get to the village where my father now lives, we have to go first to Barentu and then catch another bus to Awogaro. We have started early, hoping to be in Barentu by mid morning so we can break the back of the first part of the journey before the heat really cranks up. My brothers tell me it is four or five hours to Barentu, but they won't give me a straight answer when I ask how long from Barentu to Awogaro. The best I can get out of them is, 'It is three hours, but it can take a whole day.' The scene at the bus station is the now familiar mêlée, making me feel like a seasoned traveller. Young boys clambering all over the buses while touting for trade? No problem. Girls selling limes for travel sickness? Seen it all before. I even spot a bus with the word 'Barentu' written (in English and Tigrinya) on a piece of card in the windscreen, much to my own amazement and that of my brothers.

We pile on to the bus, which promisingly is already two-thirds full, claim our seats, and then get back off again to buy supplies. By the time we have stocked up on water, bread and fruit, the bus is full and ready to leave. Without realizing, I have become quite attached to these rickety blue buses. They are ancient Italian stock, and although I have sat on more comfortable stones, there is something very retro about them that appeals to the vintage-lover in me. These buses were once stylish and cool, and cruising along pre-war Italian cobbles they'd make for a great fashion shoot. Although judging by the state they are in now – all torn curtains and threadbare seats – I doubt they'd remember much from their early, no doubt slightly classier, days. My affection for them might also be because, despite their decrepit state and that of many of their passengers, there is still a very European feel to them, albeit a Europe of a bygone era. It's not quite like travelling on a Routemaster, but it's pretty close.

As I take my seat near the window, Medhanie and Zemichael jostle each other slightly to take the seat next to me. I let them think I haven't seen them, and smile into the window as Zemichael triumphantly lands next to me, with Medhanie to the right of him. It is about five o'clock as we lurch out of Keren. It is not yet dawn, so I follow my brothers' lead and try to grab a little more sleep. When I open my eyes the landscape is even more barren than it was between Asmara and Keren. The mountains have been replaced by a flat, arid landscape that looks even harsher for its uniformity. We pass fewer and fewer people, and the majority of our fellow travellers are soldiers. What feels like every few miles, but is probably more like every hour, the bus goes through a military checkpoint and bored soldiers get on and check everyone's identification. Anyone travelling must have a valid pass from their local government office which states where they are travelling, the relevant dates and the purpose of their trip (family visit, work, etc.). Without this authorization you will be escorted off the bus and taken to the nearest police or military holding station while officials check you are not AWOL from your national service military unit. This can take anything from a few hours to a couple of weeks, during which time you may be incarcerated at a military camp. Believe me, it is not like forgetting your driving licence and having to present it at a later date.

On the way from Asmara to Keren, I wasn't asked once for my ID card. OK, so I don't have one, but I have my passport which does the job, and besides, they don't know that. I took immediate offence each time a soldier asked everyone on the bus but me. He could at least pretend I look like a 'normal' Eritrean, I'd think to myself. It's the reverse of what happens to me at home, or whenever I go through immigration anywhere in Europe. Whenever identification of any sort is required, any black person who has grown up in a white society will always assume they will be the first, and often only, person pulled out of the queue. It's not paranoia, it's fact – or mathematical probability, if you prefer. I have spent my life justifying myself and my right to be in England to various officials. When I lost my passport a couple of years ago, the woman on the 'help line' got a little too excited when I told her my country of origin and that I had an adoption certificate rather than a birth certificate. She asked for my home phone number and address and tried to pass me on to immigration, even though I told her I'd had a valid passport before and I'd lived here for over twenty years. I was so freaked out that I hung up and only called back from a public pay phone so she couldn't trace me.

My name and distinctly middle-class English accent don't help. I forever have to convince doubting officials and others that 'Yes, I am Hannah Pool', or 'Yes, this is my credit card'. I went through a phase of carrying my passport around all the time because I was so sick of people asking to see extra identification, taking one look at my name, another at my face and then assuming the two couldn't possibly go together. So yes, I do take the whole identification business rather seriously. Only instead of feeling flattered that for once I am not assumed to be a fraud, I am miffed. Here I am on a bus full of black people and I am the only one not to be asked for ID. 'It's not fair!' I want to shout. Why am I always the odd one out? Is there nowhere in the world where I will be treated the same as everyone else?

And then I hear the magic word: 'Pass?' barks the soldier, in English. And even though I have been silently hoping for this, I am surprised by his aggressive tone. I proudly hand over my passport, but the soldier shakes it away. 'ID card,' he says.

'I don't have an ID card,' I reply, taking my sunglasses off, like the book tells me to if I'm ever talking to an official. I doubt this guy is high up in anything much, but he has an almighty rifle slung over his shoulder, which is official enough for me.

'You are Eritrean, you have ID card,' says the soldier, unimpressed.

'Yes, I am Eritrean, but I am also a British citizen – look, I have a visa in there from the Eritrean Embassy in London: will that do?' I say, mortified that I have had to resort to flagging up my 'Britishness'.

'You must have an ID card, you cannot travel without ID card,' says the soldier, not caring where I'm from – and why should he?

'I don't have one: this is my first time in Eritrea. I am adopted,' I say, opting for a different tack.

'What is this adopted?' says the soldier, getting angrier.

I look to my uncharacteristically quiet brothers for help.

'Does the visa have Tigrinya on it?' whispers a worried-looking Zemichael.

'Yes, I don't know what it says but there is definitely some Tigrinya there,' I reply, opening the passport to the page with the green visa stapled inside.

Zemichael takes it from me and shows it to the increasingly agitated soldier, who studies the tiny piece of card for an excruciating length of time, then hands it back to my brother, seemingly satisfied.

'Most of them are illiterate, but he was a clever one and he didn't want to be made to look like a fool,' says Zemichael, when the soldier is well off the bus.

'It's fine – actually it was quite exciting,' I say.

'Now you feel like a proper Eritrean?' says Zemichael, laughing and shaking his head. For the rest of the journey, whenever we stop at a checkpoint I am always asked for my ID, as are the other two women on the bus, who I am told would usually be able to get away with just giving a flash of their wedding rings (married women are exempt from national service, so their movements aren't restricted).

'It is because of the direction we are going,' explains Medhanie. 'Our father lives in the north, near the border, and they think you might be trying to escape into Sudan, and from there maybe to Europe or America.'

The bus carries on for another hour or so until we come to a standstill. There is no wire across the road, so it's not another checkpoint. 'We are taking a break,' says Medhanie. 'Do you need the toilet?' Indeed I do, but with this flat landscape I can see for miles and there certainly aren't any cafés or other buildings around, which can only mean one thing. I have been gearing myself up for this, but I'm not quite sure what the etiquette is.

I look around for some clues and see the two other women from the bus head off in the opposite direction from the men. 'Shall I follow them?' I ask, thinking out loud as much as anything else.

'Yes, you follow them, just go near where they go, and we will meet you back at the bus. Don't worry. If they say anything to you, just say *"dehaan"*, which means everything is good,' says Zemichael.

Sheepishly I follow the women as they walk away from the road. The land is so dry there aren't even any bushes around. Eventually they have obviously decided they have gone far enough away from the bus, so they squat down and lift up their long dresses. I walk a little further, not wanting to embarrass them, or perhaps myself, and then I do the same, actually thankful that I opted to wear a long skirt.

'Was it OK?' asks Medhanie as we get back on the bus. 'Yes, fine, *dehaan*,' I say, proud of how little fuss I made – not bad for someone who finds even public toilets a little too public.

At about 10 a.m., just over five hours after we set off from Keren, we pull into Barentu bus station. It's a big space, with a couple of cafés around the outskirts, and in the middle distance a military camp and hospital. Other than the military camp, Barentu's main purpose is as a stopping point for buses, soldiers and anyone else trying to go from east to west, for example aid agencies (and after five hours on a bus the UN four-wheel drives look like limousines). Prostitution is rife here, as are HIV and Aids.

'You two go and find a café, and I will find out where the bus to Awogaro goes from,' says Medhanie. Zemichael and I obediently find a café where we can sit outside so we can keep an eye out for the bus. Medhanie joins us a few minutes later and tells us that a bus should be here in a while, but we have plenty of time to have some food. We order tea and more *nai tsom*, which seems to be having the desired calming effect on my insides. We eat in near silence, tired and hungry from our early start. Once the food is gone, we have some coffee and then pay up and go to join the queue for the bus.

You know the adage about the English being good at queuing? That was obviously made up by someone who had never seen an Eritrean queue. Instead of everyone having to wait in line in the now blazing hot sun, we simply put our bags in the queue and go and find some shade nearby. The number of bags or items (coats and jumpers will do just as well) represents the number of people, so we just put three bags down, and take refuge under a nearby tree. Everyone recognizes the system, no one pushes in, and when I suggest that perhaps we should stay nearby in case someone steals our bags I am nearly laughed out of the station and reminded that 'there is no crime in Eritrea'. Still unsure, I volunteer to stay with the bags, but after only ten minutes the heat gets the better of me and I join Medhanie and Zemichael in the shade. We sit. And sit. And sit. An hour passes. Then two, three and four. The queue of bags is getting longer and longer. People, myself included, have gone from twitchy (around the two-hour mark) to resigned. Eventually a bus pulls up in front of us. There is a huge surge forward as people rush to claim their bags. I move to get up, but Medhanie tells me I am to stay with these bags; he and Zemichael will buy the tickets, get our seats, and then come back for me and get the remaining bags. After five hours of waiting I am desperate to be part of the action, so I take my frustration out on them and start harping on about how I am perfectly capable of boarding a bus on my own. But they take no notice, and by the time I have finished my rant, they are over by the bus, so I stand under the tree like a spare part. A few minutes later and I lose sight of both of them in the crush. With bus tickets flying everywhere and everyone shouting and jostling each other it looks like a miniature stock exchange trading floor. Zemichael emerges from the crowd and runs up to me. 'Medhanie has got our seats, so if you go and take his place and hold the three seats he will come back and help me with the bags,' he says, out of breath from the running. I ignore him and lift up some of the bags, but Zemichael takes them from me and tells me to go. I make a feeble attempt at arguing my case, then give up and run to find Medhanie, figuring I'll have plenty of time with them on the bus to discuss the finer points of feminism.

I get on and spot Medhanie, guarding three seats and talking to someone in the seat in front. We swap places, and he goes to help Zemichael with the bags. It transpires Medhanie's friend and his family have been waiting since 5 a.m. for a bus to Awogaro – that's pretty much a ten-hour wait, which puts our five hours in a different context. Apparently this bus wasn't even supposed to be going to Awogaro, but people complained so the driver said that for an extra 10 NK (the ticket should cost 20 NK) each he would take us there. Zemichael sits next to me, Medhanie sits with his friend on the seat in front, and an inordinate number of other people (complete with live chickens, giant bags of salt, etc.) squeeze on. Children are passed through the windows to kiss goodbye to relatives, others pass letters to the driver so he can drop them off at the villages we pass en route. After a good half an hour's commotion, the bus finally gets going. About half an hour into the journey, Zemichael asks me if I would mind if he moves seats. There is a pregnant woman holding a toddler, and because there are no seats left she is sitting on the engine. I tell Zemichael he is the only gentleman on the bus, and he swaps places with the woman. The woman immediately starts to speak to me in Tigrinya, but soon gives up and hands me her baby regardless. I put the child on my lap, and the woman heads for the back of the bus, from where she produces another child, who she sits on her lap and immediately starts to breastfeed. For the rest of the journey, the woman and I sit pretty much silently, occasionally swapping children as she feeds them in turn. It makes a pleasant change to feel useful, if mute and with a squirming child on my lap.

22

We arrive in Awogaro just after seven o'clock. The bus jerks to a stop and everyone scrambles to get off; everyone apart from me. My legs won't move. I don't want to get off the bus, just like I didn't want to get off the plane, didn't want to get out of the cab when I was with Manna, and didn't want to walk into the room where I met my birth family. I'm scared of what I'll find, of what it will be like to see how my father lives. As we've gotten nearer and nearer I have become more and more apprehensive. One thought has been in my head: when I get out of this bus I will see what my life would have been like had I not been adopted. Meeting my family in Asmara is one thing – it's romantic, a dream come true and other clichés – but coming face to face with the reality of their daily existence is another.

And yet, it was me who wanted to come here. When we'd said goodbye in Asmara that was supposed to be it, for this trip at least, and then I went and demanded that Medhanie take me to the villages. It's as if I have become addicted to these sort of situations, to the fear and sheer panic I feel when forcing myself to come face to face with people and places I have spent my life avoiding. And now I have ended up here, having ignored numerous warnings: too scared to get off the bus in my father's village.

I have lost track of how many times someone has used the phrase 'can of worms' when I have told them of my plans to come to Eritrea. The feelings I have been through since I arrived are much stronger than that, much more intense. A whole hypermarket of cans of worms might just about touch it. And yet something keeps pulling me back into the queue, asking for more. I was desperate to meet my birth family, but I didn't want to walk into the room they were in. I want to see my father's village, but I don't want to get off the bus.

The bus is now nearly empty and I can't linger inside any longer. I have passed all our bags out to my brothers, smoothed down my skirt and retied my headscarf numerous times. (Luckily I brought two headscarfs, one black, one orange and red. I put the black one on this morning only to be gently told a few hours ago by Zemichael that the only time women wear black headscarfs is when they are in mourning.) I can think of no more delaying tactics. I walk to the front of the bus. Medhanie and Zemichael have disappeared – they must be on the other side. My sunglasses make me feel invisible, even though I know that in fact they make me stand out even more than I do already, but I am glad I've got them on as within seconds I am surrounded by children, all pointing, staring and whispering, but keeping a safe distance. I spot Zemichael in the crowd, and head towards him. The children, by now confident I don't have a clue what they are saying, are circling me and shouting rather than whispering.

'Zemichael!' I shout, trying to get his attention.

'Zemichael, Zemichael, Zemichael!' shout the children, falling about laughing. Thankfully he turns around, so I don't have to say anything else. He sees the cluster of children, adopts what must be his best 'teacher' voice and waves them away: they all scatter. We find Medhanie, deep in conversation with a boy of about sixteen and two girls roughly the same age. The teenagers have distributed our bags among themselves and are carrying them – the girls on their heads, the boy in his hands.

'Hi,' I say quietly to the group. The two girls shoot each other embarrassed glances and then fix their eyes on the floor.

'Hello. Welcome,' says the boy, in a deep voice that sounds as if it has just broken.

'Thank you. I'm Hannah, who are you?' I say.

'I am Tesfit, I am your brother,' he says slowly and seriously. Medhanie and Zemichael stand there looking like proud parents.

'It is good to meet you,' I say, adding for Medhanie and Zemichael's benefit as much as his, 'your English is very good.'

The boy visibly relaxes, puts down the bags, takes hold of me and kisses me three times. When we are done with the traditional greeting I turn to the two girls, who have been watching the proceedings from a safe distance. 'So are you my sisters?' I ask, trying to sound as if it's a game. They both look at the floor again, though this time I do get a little giggle.

In among the warnings of how 'hard' I'd find village life, I have also been told to prepare for the villagers' response to me. The consensus seems to be that while a decade ago those in the villages may have never seen a white person before, these days, thanks to the presence of the UN, VSO and the like, that is no longer the case. What most villagers won't have seen is an Eritrean who dresses and sounds like a white person. 'You are like them, but you are not like them – they won't know what to think of you. They will be frightened of you at first,' is pretty much the gist of things, and judging by my first five minutes here, it's an accurate description.

'*Men semkee?*' (What is your name?) I ask, hoping speaking

Tigrinya, no matter how badly, will make them more at ease.

'Don't speak to them in Tigrinya – they speak English, they are just shy,' says Zemichael, before turning to them and saying something in Tigrinya. 'Ask them again, in English.'

'It's fine. I don't mind if they are shy – they don't have to speak English,' I reply, figuring they'll never speak to me at this rate, certainly not if it becomes like homework.

'No, it is good for them; you will be good for them to practise with.'

'What is your name?' I ask the older-looking of the two.

'Tiebe,' she whispers. I nod and smile and pretend I've heard, as I can't bear to put her through this again. I turn to the other. 'What is your name?'

'Semhar,' she replies, with a touch more confidence than her sister.

'It's lovely to meet you both,' I say, wanting to kiss them but worried they'll bolt, or at least drop the bags they've still got balanced on their heads in shock. Tiebe takes a step towards me and softly kisses my right cheek, then the left, then the right again, each time expertly tipping her head slightly, as if she were wearing nothing heavier than a straw hat. Emboldened by her sister, Semhar does the same, albeit so quickly it's as if she's kissing a hot stone, but still it's a start. Everyone then laughs openly, but not unkindly, more with a sense of relief that the awkwardness is over. The two girls walk off together, chatting animatedly, and I hang back with my brothers.

'How far is the house?' I ask, hoping my voice doesn't give away my nervousness as we pass a few round huts. I try to look inside them to get an idea of what to expect, but as there is no electricity they are dark inside.

'It is not far, just a couple of minutes,' says Medhanie. 'Are you worried?'

'Worried? No, of course not. I just wanted to know how far it is.'

'Do not be afraid. They have a good house and they have enough food,' says Medhanie, trying to reassure me. I wish I knew what he meant by 'enough food'. Does he mean just enough? Surely if he meant more than enough then that's what he'd say, especially if he knew how I was feeling. 'Enough food' is not a phrase I have ever used with regard to a person's wealth or quality of life. Every single person in my life has enough food, and it is a meaningless yardstick to me. People talk about not having 'enough space', 'enough money', 'enough holidays', but never 'enough food'. And even if they do complain about not having 'enough money' then it's in relation to buying more space, more holidays or whatever else it is they've decided they need more of.

I look ahead and see that the two girls have come to a stop outside a hut. That must be it, that must be their father's house, my father's house. I can't see an entrance, which means we must be approaching it from behind. 'Is it that one?' I ask, pointing to where my half-sisters are standing, interrupting my three brothers, who are busy catching up and not bothering to translate.

'Yes, that is our father's house,' says Medhanie.

The girls have now put down their load and disappeared inside the house, presumably to announce our arrival. No sooner have they vanished than I hear a woman singing her welcome. My father's wife, Hiwet, comes out of the house. She sees Medhanie and Zemichael, but she greets me first, with kisses and even louder singing. Then it is Medhanie and

Zemichael's turn. By the time she has finished, the other inhabitants of the house have plucked up the courage to come outside and have a proper look. One by one Hiwet gently shoves four more half-siblings in front of me – I learn one is out with the cattle – and they shyly let me kiss them while standing rigid, before taking refuge behind their mother.

It is traditional, especially in the villages, for wives to be much younger than their husbands. Ages are tricky to figure out in Eritrea, especially the further back and the more rural you go. How do you keep track of years beyond the first few when people are illiterate? My mother will have been in her early teens when she married my father. He would have been in his late twenties or early thirties. By all accounts my father remarried fairly quickly after my mother died. People don't say this as a criticism, they say it as a fact – he is a farmer, a peasant, he has to look after his cattle or his children will not eat, it is not feasible that he doesn't have another wife. I have asked my brothers what my father's second wife is like, but they are not particularly forthcoming, so I don't press them on it. I will judge for myself. But it can't be easy, can it, being a young bride and inheriting five children? Her eldest son, my half-brother Melake, tells me he is about twenty-eight, and that's just a year younger than me, so she can't have had much time to get used to being a mother to another woman's children before her own came along. And what on earth does she make of me? I might be my father's long-lost daughter, but I'm not hers.

'She is telling you to sit down,' says Medhanie, bringing me out of my thoughts. There are two beds outside which Medhanie leads me towards. It is starting to get dark, and as soon as I see the beds I realize how tired I am.

'Do you want to lie down?' asks Zemichael.

'No, I'll be fine after I've sat down,' I reply, figuring the dip in temperature as night falls will revive me a little.

'Our father is on his way back from the cattle,' says Medhanie, after a brief chat with one of the older boys. The boy runs off in the same direction we came, and Medhanie tells me he has gone to find my other brother, Stephanos, who also lives in this village. In the worry about what the village would be like I'd forgotten Stephanos would also be here. I realize just how much I am looking forward to seeing him.

'We will be eating soon, do you want to wash?' asks Zemichael.

'Aren't we waiting for Asrat before we eat?' I ask, unsure how I should refer to my father in this setting.

'No, he might be a long time; we will start to prepare and he will eat when he arrives,' replies Zemichael. 'But first you must wash.'

'OK, where do I go?' I ask.

Another extended conversation ensues, without my input, and then one of the boys gets up, mounts one of the two donkeys that are tied to nearby posts, both of which have several empty petrol cans slung over them, and wanders off, riding one donkey and leading the other with a rope. 'He is going to get you some water from the well,' says Zemichael, pre-empting yet another dumb question. I instantly feel guilty. Even though I hadn't actually requested a wash I should have known to turn down the offer; I should have realized what it would entail. I can't quite believe that without realizing it I have just sent a small child on a donkey to get me some water from a well, and I don't know whether to laugh or hate myself. 'It's fine, don't worry, it is always the children's job to get the water, don't feel bad,' says the ever-sensitive Zemichael.

We sit on the beds, my brothers and I, and as they chat I decide to give them a break from the constant translation and busy myself looking around and trying to get the girls – who are now sat to our right preparing food – to make eye contact.

After about half an hour, Stephanos appears, and so does my father. Both look younger and healthier than when I last saw them. I don't know if it's because this time I am prepared for their thinness, or if they are just more relaxed as they are on their home turf. My father, though still gaunt, looks less frail. He kisses me and starts to talk rapidly. I like it that he ignores the fact I don't speak Tigrinya and just talks to me anyway. He doesn't let my not speaking Tigrinya prevent him from saying what he needs to say. It's as if he has decided that if he says enough, surely I will understand some of it. And yet he is also one of the few elders I have met who directs questions to me through my brothers. Most of them just talk over me, not having the patience or the inclination for translation, which means it's always down to me to ask what is being said.

'Our father wants to know why you look thinner than before, have you been sick?' says Zemichael. I nod and point to my stomach, while pulling a face to imply that yes, I have. I had hoped no one would notice, but my usually cast-iron stomach has been rather more fluid of late. I was warned not to eat meat while I was here since, although it would probably be far more organic than the meat I eat at home, the enzymes would be completely different and quite possibly too much for my stomach to take. But food has been such a big part of my trip, it is how my arrival has been celebrated, and I have felt I couldn't refuse. But now the matter is out of my hands.

My frequent trips to the toilet and my not-so-discreet throwing up at the side of the road on the way here have been spotted by my brothers, and they have insisted that I don't eat any more meat for the duration of my trip. 'He wants to know what you have been eating. He says it is very important that you stay strong, it is easy to get sick in the villages,' says Zemichael, translating for my father again.

I smile and pull out the bread rolls, cheese and packet of pasta we bought in Keren to see me through the trip to the villages. My father looks pleased, and then takes the pasta, and I worry that I've made some kind of faux pas by bringing it. It does look rather ridiculous in these surroundings. My brothers have already told me that while my father's brother speaks Italian my father won't in protest at their colonialism. Asrat holds the pasta up and says something at which everyone else starts to laugh. 'He says at last we have something to be grateful to the Italians for,' says Zemichael.

23

My father's house consists of three parts. The main living area is a traditional round hut, made of mud-brick walls with a grass roof. Inside is where most of the family sleeps; a wall separates off a kitchen area. Outside the hut there is what is best described as an extension. Made of wood, with a grass roof, it provides shade in the daytime and somewhere for the animals to sleep during the night. And finally, to the right of the hut, is a low rectangular outbuilding. This is where grain, wood and other supplies are kept. It is also where I wash later, and where the eldest son sleeps. Tied up to the wooden fencing which surrounds the three buildings and a clearing in the middle are the two donkeys, along with several goats and a couple of dogs. Chickens were wandering around when I arrived, but have been put in their mini-hut, I assume for their own safety. The cattle, I am told, are out feeding, being looked after by Mebrahtu, another of my half-brothers. There is no electricity; there is water only from a well. In the rainy season, mosquitoes are everywhere and malaria is rife – Zemichael tells me that Mehari, the youngest of my half-brothers, was so sick with malaria earlier this year they feared they might lose him. I guiltily remember my own reluctance to take my malaria tablets as they were making me feel nauseous – not causing me pain, not sending me mad, just a touch of nausea that was a minor inconvenience. And now here I am sitting next to someone who nearly died because they didn't have access to the tablets I was too precious to take.

Stephanos, Hiwet and Medhanie are having a heated discussion. I have no idea what they are saying but can't help feeling a little paranoid. 'What are they arguing about?' I ask Zemichael, who is engrossed but not joining in.

'They want to kill a goat, but Medhanie is telling them you are not to eat meat.'

'They want to kill it for me? But they already killed a goat, when we first met in Asmara.'

'Yes, but they want to kill this one to celebrate you coming to your father's house. Medhanie is telling them to save it. You won't be able to eat it and they need it, they shouldn't share it with me and him, we can eat meat whenever we like, they should save it for when they really need it,' he says, standing up from where he is sitting next to me on the bed to go and provide back-up for Medhanie. I also stand up, and rather pathetically try to join in, shaking my head, pointing to my stomach and then, finally, waving a bread roll about and giving it a thumbs-up. I must look ridiculous but I don't care: the goat has suddenly come to represent everything I have and they have not. It has nothing to do with compassion for the animal. I have convinced myself that if I can stop them eating it this evening, they will have it for another day. The conversation stops. My father's wife goes inside the hut, my brothers sit down, and I assume we have won our argument. Then she comes back out with a huge knife, passes it to Stephanos, and he and two of the other boys stand up and grab the by now rather panicked goat (has it sensed what is going on?). The younger boys hold its legs, Stephanos cleanly slits its throat, and the bleating stops suddenly. At this point I turn away, trying not to look shocked. I have never seen an animal have its throat slit before. And while it was done with an almost dance-like orchestration, the three men working in complete synchronicity, I'm not sure I am ready for my first gutting. What seems like only moments later, a slab of skinned goat is brought past us and into the hut where my father's wife is, and from where the deliciously spicy aroma of what I now know is the red *berbere* spice is wafting out.

'Do you like *berbere*?' asks Melake, my eldest half-brother.

'Oh yes, I love it, and *injera* – it's just the meat that is making me sick,' I say, hoping that he understands I would do anything to be able to eat with them, and in fact my willingness to eat the same as everyone else is what has made me ill.

'Do you eat *shiro*?' he asks.

'Is that the beans?' I ask, hopefully.

'Yes, the yellow beans, that is *shiro*,' he says.

'Yes, I can eat that,' I say, enthusiastically.

'Then I will make you *shiro* and add some *berbere*, then you can eat the same as us,' he says. 'Come, I will show you how to make *shiro*.'

I am so pleased that I take his hands, give them a squeeze and thank him. Thankfully, he looks pleased too, squeezes me back, lets go of one hand and then leads me with the other to sit on one of two low stools over a small steel stove that is outside. Although gender divisions are usually very strict in Eritrea, because all the men have done their national service they are adept at cooking. Melake starts to chop onions and fry them in a pan. He adds a small tin of tomato purée, the *berbere* and then the powdered bean paste. As we sit over the stove we chat. I warm to him instantly. He is the closest in age to me of everyone here. I am the break in the link and he is where the connection starts again – is that why there is no awkwardness? The concept of half-siblings doesn't seem to be relevant here. Medhanie and Zemichael refer to Melake as their brother, which means he is my brother also. Had I not been taken away we would have grown up side by side, and cooking together would have been the norm. He is on leave from his national service because he is due to get married soon, and here he is, showing me how to cook *shiro* just so I won't feel left out when they sit down to their *injera* and meat. Once he has finished adding the ingredients and the demonstration is over, we sit there quietly as Melake stirs the *shiro*. Every so often he hands me the spoon and I imitate him, stirring slowly, twice clockwise, twice anticlockwise, and then I hand the spoon back. Sitting here over this stove, the two of us not saying anything, is the closest I have felt to anyone for days.

The two girls walk past us carrying a large flat basket full of *injera*. 'Come, the meat is also ready,' says Tiebe. Melake and I get up and join the others. A large metal tray covered with *injera* is laid out before me. The *shiro* is put on top. I am about to tuck in when, luckily, I notice the bowed heads. I bow mine and my father starts to pray. A few moments later, everyone starts to eat. I am sitting next to my father and he starts to heap yet more *shiro* on top of my *injera*. There is no way I can eat all this in one sitting. I am about to protest when he starts to speak. 'He is going to eat with you. He will not have meat, he will have the *shiro* that his son and daughter made together,' says Zemichael.

It is twilight by the time we have finished eating. The moon is getting bright, but most of our light comes from the cinders in the stove and the two lanterns we have lit. We also have two torches, but they are for middle-of-the-night trips to the toilet when the lanterns have gone out. You can hear people in the neighbouring hut, which is about fifty metres away, but you can't see them, just the dim orange glow of their stove.

After we eat, coffee is served and the younger children drift off into the hut. I decide it is probably a good idea to figure out exactly where the toilet is while the others are up, just in case I have any problems. All this outdoor-by-candlelight stuff is appealing to my romantic side right now, but I might feel a bit differently in a few hours when everyone has gone to sleep. 'Where should I go to the toilet?' I ask Medhanie, knowing what his response will be.

'Come, I will show you,' he says, jumping up as I knew he would. He hands me one of the torches and leads me away from the front of the hut and past another couple of clearings. The ground is dry, treeless and littered with animal bones where the dogs have been eating. 'I'm walking across bones, wearing Birkenstocks, and I'm not freaking out,' is all I can think. We are on the outskirts of this cluster of huts, and after we walk past what looks like the last hut in the village, Medhanie says, 'You can go anywhere from here onwards,' and points out towards the disappearing horizon. I'm not sure how to reply to his grand gesture, so I just say, 'Great, thanks,' lingering where I am, unsure how to proceed. 'I will walk this way, further than you. When you have finished, turn your torch on and I will come and find you,' says Medhanie. 'OK,' I say, grateful to have the male/female etiquette explained.

I don't know what I had expected, but it's not really that bad. There is no smell. No open sewer. It's just a case of finding a spot – a low bush or a dip in the land perhaps – and squatting down. I guess I thought there'd be a special area or

193

field that the whole village used, which would be pretty stinky. But you just need to walk a polite distance past the last hut in your part of the village, and if you've brought tissue paper to use, cover it up afterwards so it doesn't fly away. In fact, once I get over my blushes, and the bones, I'd choose this over the toilets at Glastonbury any day.

When I'm finished I stand up, turn the torch on, and wave it in the direction Medhanie headed. A couple of minutes later he appears and we make our way back to the hut. In the short time we have been away, night-time has fallen. The sky, now full of stars, has gone from a deep blue to black. There are even fewer lanterns dotted about and, other than my torch, the only real light comes from the brightness of the moon.

We walk back into our clearing, and I see that the two beds everyone was sitting on have been moved underneath the 'extension'. One has been made up with sheets we brought with us from Keren, the other has my sleeping bag laid on it. Medhanie, Zemichael and I are sleeping outside. For some inexplicable reason, given my history of hating all things covered by the word 'nature', I am thrilled, if a little apprehensive. My father tells me to come inside if I get cold. I assure him I will, and my two brothers promise him they will look after me. A week or so ago I would have found this unbearably patronizing, but now I find it touching. Having examined my sleeping bag and satisfied himself that I will be warm enough, my father says his goodnights and goes inside the hut. Medhanie and Zemichael then get into one bed, and I get into the other. We blow out the last remaining lantern and lie there in the dark, chatting like children on a camping trip. Maybe it's all this fresh air, maybe it's the fact things are so very different here, but being in the village for just a few hours seems to have had a calming, sedative effect. I am happy and relaxed.

I only wake once during the night, and at first I assume it is the dogs barking or another animal I can't place that has woken me. And then I realize my father has come outside and is covering me with his *gabi*. I turn and whisper *'yekanyeley'*, 'thank you' in Tigrinya. I have no way of knowing if he has heard me or not, because he silently goes back inside. I pull the *gabi* tighter around me and wonder if I am dreaming.

24

In my new-found enjoyment of being outdoors, I had forgotten that when you sleep outside, you wake when everything else does. It's about five o'clock when I wake up to the sound of dogs, cockerels and donkeys. I have slept remarkably well and feel far fresher than is decent for this time of the morning. I look around and see Medhanie and Zemichael are not in their bed, so I turn the other way, tangling myself up in something. It is my father's *gabi*.

To my left, my brothers, my father and pretty much everyone is sitting around wrapped in white *gabis* drinking tea. '*Dehaando hadirkum*,' (Good morning), I attempt, in Tigrinya. They all laugh, but kindly, and Melake passes me a glass full of sweet tea. I wonder if he has made it his duty to look after me while I stay here, or if he has been instructed. 'Did you sleep well?' he asks.

'Yes, very well.'

'Would you like some bread?' says Medhanie, not waiting for my answer, but passing me a heavy lump of bread.

'Did the animals keep you awake?' asks Zemichael.

'No, not at all, though there was a dog or a cow or something that I kept hearing.'

'Ah, the hyenas,' says Zemichael.

We sit around for a while, then get up, although as I slept in my clothes this just involves washing my face, brushing my teeth and tying my hair back. The dawn chill has lifted surprisingly quickly, and I've got a real buzz from sleeping outside and the fact I didn't create a fuss about going to the toilet the evening before. 'Today we will visit Stephanos and his family,' says Medhanie. We sit around some more and then make our way to my brother's house on the other side of the village. Walking through the village it becomes apparent that the relaxed way my father and his family have treated me is the exception rather than the rule. Children stumble over each other trying to get a better look at me, at the same time not wanting to come too close. My brothers are quick to reply on my behalf to those who shout out at me. When I ask them what is being said, they tell me it's nothing to worry about, they are just being curious, not malicious. I ask Zemichael what they are replying, and he says, 'We just tell them we are your brothers and that you are Asrat's daughter. That is enough for them. Then they know you are not a stranger.'

We walk through the middle of the village, an area which has a row of huts (shops, I think) and cafés, past the remains of a tin mine and up a hill. Medhanie is telling me about the time last year when Stephanos was 'visited by an elephant'. I haven't seen any elephants on my trip so far, so I'm convinced he is teasing me, especially after they were so amused at how shocked I was to realize I'd been listening to hyenas all night. But even if they are teasing, I don't mind, in fact I like it – it has an edge of closeness to it. Medhanie is in the middle of promising he is telling the truth, when two little girls, one about five and one about seven, come running up to him. He bends down and effortlessly scoops up one in each arm. After kissing them both, he passes the youngest over to me. I give her a kiss on each cheek and instead of wriggling away from me, as every other child here has done, she puts her arms around my neck and kisses me back.

This, I later learn, is my niece, Nardos Stephanos. She is six years old and has charmed me instantly, not least because she doesn't seem scared of me – far from it. When her weight becomes too much and I have to put her down, she grabs my hand and leads me into her house. Inside are her two brothers, Hagos (fourteen) and Yonas (ten), her other sister, Yordanos (three), her mother (who is heavily pregnant) and my brother, Stephanos. I have realized that when visiting people's homes, children are the key. Though shy at first, they are much less wary of me than the adults, and what makes children laugh in one part of the world works just as well in another, regardless of any language barrier. Children are also much more sympathetic. No child will chastise me for not speaking 'my mother's tongue' – instead, like Nardos and her sister Fiori, they will spend an entire afternoon trying to teach me to count to ten. Stephanos' house is a traditional hut like my father's, but much smaller, and though there are chickens, there don't appear to be any other animals. My brother is a soldier so he is away most of the time, leaving his wife to look after the children. They are confident and a delight to be around, so they must be happy. They are eager to show off their English, which means they must be going to school. And yet there is something about them that makes me feel terribly sad. It's not just that they are so very small for their age, nor is it that I know how hard it must be for their mother, now pregnant with her sixth, to keep them fed. It's that despite the hardships, they have something I have never had. They are slap bang in the middle of a normal, happy Eritrean childhood. By the time I was Nardos' age, I had lost my natural mother to childbirth, my adoptive mother had taken an overdose and I was living in Norway with my third and by no means final family. Two years later I was finally settled, living in England with my dad, trying desperately to replace a Norwegian accent with a Mancunian one. My nieces and nephews have never left their village. I can see how poor they are, I can see how hard their lives will be and what little opportunity they will have, yet I am jealous of their few certainties. And I hate myself for it. What kind of a person feels jealous of a six-year-old living in poverty? I look at Nardos and think, 'This is what an Eritrean childhood looks like.' And then I ask myself, if I had the money, would I be doing this child a favour by taking her back to the UK with me or would I be screwing her up for ever?

We spend the whole day at my brother's house, and for the first time I feel relaxed enough after lunch to have a nap along with the others. Late in the afternoon we wander back to my father's house and drink yet more coffee.

If you're not looking after something, be it cattle, crops or children, there isn't much to do in the villages. While my family thought I would find the villages too hard, my friends in Asmara were divided as to whether I would love or hate village life. 'You will be bored' was one consensus; 'You will relax a little' was the other – largely depending on how they found it themselves when they were in the villages. It is hard seeing how my family live, but I am definitely relaxed rather than bored, though I am not sure if I am enjoying the slower pace of village life because it is too soon for me to be bored by it, or because I actually rather like it.

'Is it better to be poor and in the villages or poor and in the cities?' I ask my brothers later that evening when we are getting ready for our second night sleeping outside. 'It depends,' says

Medhanie. 'In general, it is better to be poor in the villages because your neighbours will help you to survive. But during the rainy season, aid cannot reach some villages, which means you are cut off from all help.'

The next morning Medhanie wakes me at about five with tea and bread. I reach for my glasses and look around for the rest of my bags. 'We are leaving after this tea,' he announces when I ask if he knows where my things are. 'Zemichael is on the bus already holding our seats.'

Dazed that we are leaving so suddenly, I don't even have time to get angry that once again I have been told what is happening, rather than asked for my opinion. I get up and start to roll up my sleeping bag, but Tesfit takes over, and I don't bother to argue. 'Do I have time to say goodbye to everyone, and maybe take a few photographs?' I ask Medhanie.

Sensing that it will probably be quicker to let me take my pictures than try to talk me out of it, Medhanie sets about rounding the family up. To my dismay, Melake has gone to help Zemichael with the bags, but otherwise everyone is there. I take some pictures of my father and his family outside their hut. Medhanie takes a couple of me alongside them, and then we start to say goodbye, to the children first, and then to my father's wife. I am about to say goodbye to my father when a white minibus pulls up nearby and Zemichael jumps out of it. Ever since we arrived I have been wanting to ask my brothers if I should give my father some money, and if so how I should go about it. For some reason I find Zemichael easier to talk to about such things, probably because, due to his time in Dekemhare, he has a sense of how hard it is trying to slot into a family full of people you don't know. He picks up on things that others don't, like how hard it is remembering everybody's names when there is just one of you and lots of them.

I run up to Zemichael, hoping to get to him before everyone else does, not that it matters too much as neither my father nor his wife will be able to understand what I am saying, though it would feel disrespectful somehow to discuss this right in front of them. 'Zemichael, should I give Asrat some money?' I ask, feeling awkward just saying it.

'Yes, but only if you have some,' he replies, in an understanding tone.

'Yes, I brought some with me, but I didn't want to offend him.'

'How do you offend people by giving them money?' asks Zemichael.

I suddenly feel foolish, and ashamed of myself. It is obvious my father needs money, and I nearly let my own, very British awkwardness get in the way. 'How much should I give?' I ask.

'Give whatever you can, he will be grateful. But you must not worry so much. It is very difficult for people who come from outside to see how we live in the villages. It looks very hard and it is only natural to want to help. But you must not feel bad. By coming back you have given our father everything he could wish for, you have brought his family back together again,' says Zemichael, and then he shouts across to my father to come and join us. We form a small huddle and Zemichael takes the money I have given him and hands it to my father. My father nods his head, takes the money and then starts to speak, pointing skywards as he does so. 'He is saying whenever he looks at the sun he will think of you. He says he is a very old man, you must come back and visit him in his home again soon. God took two daughters away and now God has given him one daughter back. He says he is not sad to say goodbye because now he has met you he knows you will come back.' And with that, my father kisses me several times on each cheek, walks back to his family and gives us a wave. Zemichael lifts up both our hands and waves for me. As we turn around and head for the bus I am fighting back the tears.

25

A couple of days later I am back in Asmara, still feeling a little down. I thought I'd gotten to grips with Eritrea, and now I realize all I'd gotten to grips with was the city, and all cities are pretty much alike once you strip them back to their bare essentials. I am still charmed by Asmara – its faded art deco look, its beaten-up cars, its palm-tree-lined main street – but Asmara is not where I am from. I am not even from Keren, for Keren is also a city. I am from the villages.

Medhanie calls my hotel, leaving a message that cheers me up. 'Sister Hannah, tomorrow we will go to our sister Timnit's village for the wedding of Timnit's daughter. I will meet you at the hotel at 6 a.m. Bring some good walking shoes, we will walk from Timnit's to our village of birth. Your brother Medha.' At last I will see where I was born, and there's a wedding thrown in – what a result.

Sure enough, on the dot of six o'clock the next morning Medhanie appears in the hotel reception. We walk to the bus station (I actually know the way!) and board one of the old Italian blue buses. Medhanie is surprised by how excited I am about going to another village so soon. I try to explain that although I found it hard, and upsetting, going to my father's village, that doesn't mean I didn't enjoy it. And that I'm looking forward to seeing where Timnit lives, but mostly I'm excited about seeing Bekishemnok – the village I was born in. 'Were we all born in Bekishemnok? You, Zemichael, the others?' I ask, for some reason hoping that the answer will be yes.

'Yes, we were all born there,' says Medhanie.

'How far is it from Timnit's village?'

'About six kilometres.'

'Do you know what that is in miles?' I ask, knowing this will make him smile, since I ask it whenever Medhanie gives me a distance.

'No,' he says, laughing, 'I am a proper statistician, I do not do miles, only kilometres like the rest of the world.'

I do mock outrage, which makes him laugh even more, and then he says, 'It will take two or three hours on foot. Bekishemnok is a very small village – the bus does not stop there. We will go first to Timnit's, then after we have rested for a day we will go to Bekishemnok.'

'Will we sleep there?'

'No, we will see our home, visit our relatives and then walk back to Timnit's.'

Our home? Without realizing it, I had assumed our home no longer existed. 'What do you mean, "our home"? Is the hut still there?' I ask, wanting to be sure I'm on the right lines.

'Yes, of course our home is still there. We still own it, but our father lets another family use it.'

'The exact same hut?'

'Yes, but it's not a hut, it's a *hidmo*.' Medhanie clocks my blank look. 'In the highlands they have *hidmos*, not huts. So our father lives in a hut, but our sister lives in a *hidmo*, and we were all born in *hidmos*.'

'I know this is a stupid question, but what's the difference?' I ask, figuring it's better to ask Medhanie now than get it wrong in front of others later.

'A *hidmo* is bigger than a hut; it's made of mud and stone, with wooden poles inside to hold it up. The roof is usually timber with earth on top to make it waterproof. *Hidmos* can have separate rooms. They last for many generations, much longer than huts. Everything in our *hidmo* is the same as it was when we left, it's just a different family living there.'

'But different furniture, different chairs, different beds?'

'Different stools, yes, but the exact same bed. The bed you were born on.'

And then we both go quiet, neither of us, for the sake of the other, wanting to take the conversation to its conclusion: the bed where our mother died.

The journey to Timnit's is five of the bumpiest hours I've ever spent. The road seems to disappear at regular intervals, not that it bothers the driver, who is just as happy hurtling along a rocky dust path as smooth tarmac. I decide to pull my window curtain across, not to stop the sun blazing in but to stop me seeing just how dangerously we are travelling. Medhanie and I are not the only people on the way to Timnit's – Zerai (the cousin with the twinkly eyes), Amehatzion (my father's brother) and to my delight his wife (perhaps I'll ask her about my mother later in the journey), and one of their daughters and her two children are all on their way to the wedding too. I ask if my father is going to join us there, but it turns out Melake is also getting married this weekend, so the family is split in half. We are going to Timnit's, and Zemichael, Stephanos and my father are going to the other wedding. People are clearly not happy about the split, but it is better this way than to have everyone at one and no one at the other. All this talk of weddings and divided loyalties actually makes me feel quite at home. In fact, I'm looking forward to the wedding for more than girlie, sentimental reasons – it will be a nice change to watch from the sidelines while someone else is the centre of attention.

We arrive at Dersseney, my sister's village, in the early evening. Timnit is as thrilled to see me as I am her. We hug and kiss and then she takes me into her house, a traditional *hidmo* that is much larger than my father's hut. Inside, the walls are lined with people, a few of whom I recognize from the bus. They are sitting on logs or stools, or just crouching down. There must be about twenty or thirty people in here, eating, and drinking, and someone somewhere is drumming. As we enter the room, Timnit steers me to a group of mostly middle-aged women (some older, some younger). Timnit starts to sing and dance, a sort of hop from foot to foot, with a shuffle back and forth in time to the drum, which I still haven't managed to locate. The women all stand up and join in, singing, clapping and dancing around me. I feel like a moron just standing there, so I do my best to copy them, at which point the circle opens up a little and a woman in her mid to late thirties comes in front of me. She is holding a hand drum, made of what looks like wood and cowhide, and her hands are moving so quickly they make me feel dizzy. I try to show my appreciation by dancing even more enthusiastically, but by now I am exhausted, not to mention a little over-whelmed. In fact, I think I might faint. I look for the nearest thing to sit on, spy an empty stool, and dance towards it, all the while slowing my movements and making apologetic 'I'm tired' actions. I sit down, just seconds before I would have fallen. So much for not being the centre of attention.

After some food – *shiro* and *injera* – and some sweet tea, I feel much better, but things are no quieter in the house.

Apparently many of the people coming for the wedding have come today so they can help with the preparations – it's kind of like a rehearsal dinner. One hut is full of women making *suwa*, a kind of Eritrean home brew. Another has women making a mountain of *injera* and chopping vegetables, and then outside there is what keeps being described to me as the *das* or 'wedding hut' – this is what I thought was some sort of an extension in my father's house. It is, sort of, but it's temporary, put up when there is a wedding, for guests to sit under. Like my father's (which I now realize was for his son's wedding), Timnit's is made mostly of wooden fencing, but instead of grass, this roof is made from stitched-together empty grain bags, through which you can see the words, 'A gift from the USA'. Finally, there is a rectangular brick building, similar to my father's outbuilding but with a corrugated-iron roof. I am told this is where the schoolteacher lives, and it is where Medhanie and I are sleeping. Someone has already laid out my sleeping bag on top of one of the two beds in the room. There is another bed, a small table, and on the walls a few pictures ripped out of old magazines, which are curling at the edges. Judging by the pictures – sewing patterns, make-up advertisements and the like – this is a woman's room. Medhanie's things are on the other bed and someone has lit the lantern on the table.

As I put my bag down, Medhanie enters the room. 'Did you eat with the women?' he asks, looking pleased with himself.

He must have been glad to be rid of me if only for an hour or so, I think.

'Yes, and I danced too,' I reply.

'That is good, you will have made Timnit very happy.'

At that moment, Timnit enters the room, followed by three of the women who were dancing with her earlier and one of her daughters. She is speaking rapidly to Medhanie, who looks a little stunned but seems to be agreeing with what she is saying. Medhanie turns to me and says, 'Timnit has just heard that we plan to go to Bekishemnok tomorrow. She doesn't want us to go.'

I interpret this as Timnit wanting to spend as much time with me as possible, and perhaps worrying we will miss the wedding. I tell Medhanie to tell her we are only going to Bekishemnok for the day.

'She still doesn't want you to go; she says you will not manage the walk,' says Medhanie.

I smile reassuringly and say, 'Tell her I am stronger than I look: I will be fine.'

Whatever Medhanie says, it doesn't have the calming effect intended. Timnit is talking even more excitedly now. She pauses for a moment to let Medhanie relay her thoughts. 'She says you are not going to Bekishemnok. You will go next time. That is the end of the matter.'

Now it is me who is stunned. I have come to expect surprise at my desire to go to Bekishemnok, but I never for a moment imagined I'd be told outright that I couldn't go.

'Why doesn't she want me to go?' I ask.

'She says your home is here, with her. All there is in Bekishemnok is soil and dirt,' says Medhanie, shrugging his shoulders in a way that implies he agrees with Timnit and, if anything, is relieved that the trip is now off.

So that's how things go in this family, I think: it's Timnit who wears the trousers – sweet, traditional Timnit.

All the others have tried to put me off going to Bekishemnok, but no one has actively forbidden me from going, not even my father, until now. And there was I thinking that because Timnit was the only woman in the family she'd have little or no say about anything. I am of course pleased to be wrong, but that poses me something of a problem as far as my trip to Bekishemnok is concerned. Medhanie is acting as if now that Timnit has spoken there is no debating the issue, and the other women who are in the room are chatting among themselves and also clearly in agreement.

'It is OK, we will go next time,' says Medhanie, trying to appease me.

Is it because Timnit is older than him, because she's his sister, or just because she has the stronger personality that he has caved in so quickly, and assumes I will do the same? It can't be because he doesn't want to go – sure, he was reluctant at first, but only a few hours ago on the bus he was saying how much he was looking forward to it.

'I don't want to go next time, I want to go this time. Tell Timnit that I am going tomorrow,' I say, not caring that I sound like a spoilt brat. Is that a gasp or a ripple of laughter from the women watching as Medhanie translates?

Timnit starts to reply to Medhanie, then gives up on the translation altogether and turns to me. She is talking even faster and with more passion; she is also waving her hands in my face. I may not understand her words, but I know what she is saying.

When she pauses for breath, I start talking, this time directly to Timnit, and not waiting for Medhanie to translate. 'I know you don't want me to go, but I have to. I have waited thirty years for this. Imagine if you had never seen Bekishemnok, never seen the place you were born, and I told you not to go?

209

I have promised it to myself and I am going, but I would like it to be OK with you.'

Timnit replies, this time briefly, but again she does so directly to me, not to Medhanie.

'I'm going,' I respond adamantly.

She shakes her head, and her hands for added emphasis, and says something to me. I may not understand Tigrinya but I know clipped tones when I hear them, and besides you don't have to be much of a linguist to realize that while I am standing there saying, 'I'm going,' she is replying, 'You're not,' albeit in a different language.

We carry on like this for a few minutes, me speaking in English, Timnit in Tigrinya, Medhanie sitting redundantly on his bed. The other women are clearly enjoying the spectacle (I am beginning to get the impression no one takes on Timnit), but Medhanie's looking like he'd rather be anywhere else. Has he never seen two women argue before? And then it clicks, and I feel myself let a smile slip as I realize that despite our language difference, despite the fact we grew up thousands of miles apart and despite the fact we barely know each other, Timnit and I are arguing in exactly the same way. Suddenly my trip to Bekishemnok doesn't seem so important. 'Timnit,' I say, holding up my hands in mock defeat. And then Timnit's face also cracks, and we both start to laugh. She grabs my right hand in hers, and puts her left arm around my shoulder, kissing me on the right cheek as she does so. She then speaks, and I know she is telling me it's OK if I go. Poor old Medhanie is still sitting on the bed, looking left out, but also relieved we have stopped arguing. 'She says you can go,' he says.

'I know, I know, and I am sorry if we upset you by arguing,' I reply, pulling him up to join us in a three-way hug.

'It is OK,' he says, and then a few seconds later he adds: 'I think I just saw what it would have been like growing up with the two of you.'

26

I am woken by the sound of someone opening the door to our room. It is Mehawi, Timnit's second-eldest son, and my nephew. Like Melake, my father's eldest in Awogaro, Mehawi seems to be looking after me during my stay here in Dersseney. He is carrying tea and bread, which he sets down on the table in the middle of the room.

'Good morning, my aunt. Did you sleep well?' he asks.

Hearing this sweet yet awkward adolescent call me his aunt so tenderly nearly breaks my heart. Is it me he is shy of, or speaking English? I wonder what he makes of me, this seventeen-year-old? In the space of a couple of weeks I've gone from having no nephews or nieces, to suddenly having thirteen, with another on the way.

'I slept very well, thank you. How did you sleep, Mehawi?' I say, slowly, hoping it will help his confidence if he can understand me.

'I slept very well,' he replies, bringing me a glass of tea and the bread.

Medhanie turns over. 'Good morning,' he says, cheerfully.

'Good morning,' we reply.

Medhanie speaks to Mehawi in Tigrinya and then starts laughing. 'Timnit has sent him to go to Bekishemnok with us to make sure that we come back,' he says.

I have been told the walk to my village will take anything between two and four hours. It is over rocky semi-desert, and there is no road. Although some of the flatter parts of the walk are worn down by time to form a path, for the most part it's a case of scrabbling over rocks and dodging cacti. In my stupid 'traveller' way, I'm looking forward to the walk, and to proving to everyone that I can do it, and that I am as strong as they are. As the three of us set off, it becomes clear that, despite last night's reticence, Medhanie is still looking forward to seeing the village where he was born, and he tells me he hasn't been there for six or seven years. The three of us fall into an easy banter, the conversation switching from Tigrinya to English but in such a relaxed way that for once I don't feel excluded. And besides, most of the time I'm too busy struggling to either keep up or figure out where to put my feet so I don't slip on the rocks and break my ankle. Despite our early start, after about twenty minutes of walking the sun is already making things harder, as is the litre bottle of water I am carrying. The others have offered to carry the water, but as I need to swig from it every few minutes I'd rather carry it myself. I hate to admit it, and I certainly won't to anyone who asks, but I'm finding the going tougher than I'd expected. The novelty of walking past a cactus several times taller than myself has fast worn off, as has the tomboyish appeal of scrabbling over rocks, which started off making me feel intrepid, but now is just making me feel knackered. About an hour into the walk, Medhanie and Mehawi stop at the top of a particularly large boulder. Though grateful, I am mildly annoyed that they might think I need a break.

'Why are we stopping? I'm fine to go on,' I say, with faux energy.

'Come, stand up here with us,' says Medhanie, pulling me up to join them.

The view is amazing. I have been so busy trying to make sure I didn't slip that I have barely looked up. Up close the landscape looks plain and rocky, with only the occasional bright pink of a flowering cactus to brighten things up, but on a grand scale, the effect is breathtaking. The sheer size of such a repetitive and harsh landscape turns it into a thing of beauty. All around, I can see the small terraces built into the mountains to stop the rain from disappearing, which give some of them the appearance of having tree rings, adding to the dramatic effect.

'Can you see that white dot?' says Medhanie, pointing straight ahead, into the far distance.

'Yes, just about.'

'Well, that is the church in Bekishemnok,' he says, pausing to make sure I can indeed see it. 'They paint the churches white so it guides you to the village, and if you look around the church you should be able to see the houses. One of those is our home, the place we were all born,' he says, proudly.

I look, but other than a vague sense of a couple of roof tops, I can't really make anything out, other than the fact it seems we've got a way to go yet.

Trying my best to hide how fazed I am by how far away the village still seems, I take a couple of photographs from the top of the boulder, not least because I know none of my friends will ever believe I managed to walk that far without hailing a cab. Refreshed by the break, I start to walk with new vigour. Now I have had my first glimpse of my village, its church dangling temptingly on the horizon in front of me, I am even more desperate to see it properly. It is only the heat, and of course the damn rocks, that stop me breaking into a run.

About twenty minutes further along, the rocks give way to a narrow path, which Medhanie tells me winds its way down pretty much all the way to the church, give or take a couple of rocky bits in between. He tells me we are making good time, and that if we do it in under three hours, which we look likely to, he will be very impressed with me. Just as he is telling me that I obviously have Eritrean blood as otherwise I wouldn't be able to do this walk so easily, an elderly-looking woman, carrying a heavy bundle on her back and a chicken by its feet and keeping the sun off her head with a black umbrella, and a younger man come into view on the path ahead. These are the first people we have met since we left Timnit's at eight o'clock this morning. As the two draw nearer, it is obvious Medhanie knows them. When they are close by, he rushes up to them and excitedly greets them both. I see now that the woman isn't that old, just hunched with the weight of the load she is carrying on her back, and the chicken, to my surprise, is very much still alive. The woman takes one look at me, gasps and pretty much drops her umbrella (though not the chicken). She covers her free hand with her mouth as if in shock and then starts talking furiously in Tigrinya with Medhanie. She gasps at pretty much everything he is saying, and then starts to kiss me on alternate cheeks and raise her hands to the sky, chicken and all.

'Is she a relative?' I ask Medhanie, in between being hugged and kissed by the woman.

'Yes, they are both our relatives; they are on their way to Timnit's for the wedding,' he says.

'How are we related?' I ask, figuring it must be pretty close going by the strength of this woman's hugs.

'She is our father's wife's sister,' says Medhanie.

'Our stepmother's sister?' I ask, surprised that she is not a blood relative given the strength of her response.

'Yes,' says Medhanie. The woman lets go of me for a second, steps backwards, and hands the chicken, which by now is flapping as if its life depended on it, to her male companion. She then turns back to me and starts to speak as she brings her hands up and strokes my face, and as she does this she is also crying, sobbing even. The only words I pick up are the by now familiar *'yesmesgin'* (thank you / I am satisfied) and 'Hidat'.

'Medhanie, whose sister is she?' I ask, on hearing my mother's name.

'Our father's wife's sister?' he says again, but this time it is more of a question than a statement of fact.

'Is she the sister of our father's wife now, our stepmother in Awogaro, or the sister of our father's first wife, Hidat?' I ask.

'I am sorry, now I am getting confused. I do not understand this stepmother business,' says Medhanie.

'It's fine, it's just that she seems very upset, and I thought I heard her say my mother's name, Hidat,' I reply.

'Yes she did, she is Hidat's sister,' says Medhanie, in a eureka sort of tone. 'She is the sister of our father's first wife,' he continues, slowly and precisely.

'She is my mother's sister?' I say, wanting to be absolutely sure I've got it right. I have not yet met any of my mother's relatives and I want to be sure if this is the first one.

'Yes,' says Medhanie, in a satisfied tone.

'Did she know I was going to be at the wedding?' I ask.

'No – she knew we'd found you but that was all. She is crying because she is so happy; she says seeing you here standing on this path in front of her is like God has brought her sister back to her.'

This is the first time I have thought of myself as the daughter of someone else's sister. As the continuation of something. It is also the first time I have thought of my mother in such a way, as a sibling, rather than solely as a mother and wife. But of course she lived most of her life before she was a mother. And this is the first time I have thought of how hard her death must have been not just for her husband and children, but for her family and those who had known her for the longest.

One of my main reasons for coming to the villages was the feeling that I would never get any real information about her from the people I had met so far. I had tried to ask my father, but it felt wrong in Asmara, like I was bringing a downer on the celebrations by bringing her up. I had tried in Awogaro, but again it felt wrong, especially in front of his new family. I had tried with my siblings, but, as with my father, I was put off by their reluctance. The only person who had told me anything of any substance so far was the wife of my father's brother, who had also been my mother's best friend. So although I'd told everyone I wanted to come to Bekishemnok to see the place I was born, a large part of that desire was the hope I would learn things about my mother on the way. And here I am, on a path in the middle of nowhere, standing in front of my mother's sister.

The five of us have been standing around in near silence for a few moments. Every so often my aunt mutters something, and then perhaps sensing we need to be on our way, she kisses me (again) and goes to kiss Medhanie and Mehawi. As we say goodbye, and give plenty of assurances that we will be back in Dersseney in time for the wedding, she tries to give me her umbrella. 'She wants you to take it, to protect yourself from the sun,' says Medhanie.

'Tell her thank you very much, but I am fine. She needs it more than I do and I will not take it from her,' I say.

Medhanie says something to her, but she ignores him and tries to hand me the umbrella regardless. My newfound aunt may not be as elderly as I first thought but I still reckon she's in her early sixties, and the sun is now punishingly hot. I push the umbrella back towards her as forcefully as I can without seeming rude and then do an exaggerated impression of someone who enjoys the sun. She laughs and then shakes her head and eventually acquiesces. She then turns to the man she is with, who has been watching events unfold from a safe distance, chicken in hand, and motions for him to come forward. He greets me politely, and I assume he is her son but cannot be sure. Then we head off in opposite directions, and as she walks away I can hear her muttering 'Hidat' and *yemesgin*.

We walk quietly for a while, Medhanie and Mehawi chatting to each other, my stomach doing somersaults, the voice inside my head saying, 'I just met my mother's sister' over and over.

27

'Can you see the *hidmos* now?' asks Medhanie, breaking the flow of Tigrinya that has been the background to my thoughts.

I look up and realize that somehow we now only have one field to cross and the *hidmos* are already above us. 'I can see them – so do we just have to walk through that sandy field?' I ask.

'Yes, but it is not a field, it is a dry river,' says Medhanie.

Fifteen minutes later, and we are on the edge of the village. I have been told to expect a village much smaller than either my father's or Timnit's, and one that is not in a good way. Most people, like my father, left in 1981 when the war got too close. There is little left in the village, just a cluster of about twenty *hidmos* built into a hill, the inhabitants of which are either very old, very young or those looking after either group. Everyone else leaves as soon as they can.

Medhanie points to a house near the top of the village. 'That's it, that is our home,' he says, before breaking into an excited skip.

I stop about twenty metres in front of the *hidmo*. My stomach feels hollow, as if I've just been punched, as I stand there, rooted to the spot, trying to take in what I am doing, as much as what I am seeing: I am standing in front of the place I was born in. In a few minutes I will be inside, and a few minutes after that I will be in the spot my mother died.

Medhanie has already established that the family who now use the *hidmo* are not in, so he and Mehawi have gone to find them, which leaves me able to stand outside, on my own, and approach it in my own time. Although it is a traditional *hidmo*, made of stone and mud, with a wood-and-earth roof, it's a rectangle rather than a circle. The stones on the outside are the same kind we have just spent two and a half hours negotiating. The house looks pretty big from the outside, which I guess it would have to be given that at one time there were at least seven occupants. I suddenly wonder if it was such a good idea to come here. How could it not be upsetting, how could I not expect to be weirded out? Perhaps I should have listened to everyone: there must be a reason why Medhanie hasn't been here for years, and why Timnit was adamant I shouldn't come. I'd put both down to their sense of having moved on, a sense that I didn't think I could ever achieve without coming here, but perhaps I misjudged them. Perhaps they knew how coming here would make me feel and were trying to protect me.

Medhanie and Mehawi are back, followed by a frail-looking woman who is bent double with age. 'Her family live here now; she is going to make us tea and show us around the house,' says Medhanie cheerfully. I take strength from him – if he's not upset or freaked out, why should I be?

I step into the cool darkness of the *hidmo*. Medhanie immediately starts to walk around, oohing and aahing as he points to what few things are dotted around, as if reunited with friends. I stand there wondering what I am feeling. I'm not so away with the fairies that I'd expected to actually recognize anything, but I can't help checking myself for any sense of familiarity, anything at all. The old woman motions for us to sit on the log behind us, which gives me a better view of the room, and means I don't have to walk around, which was making me feel like I was in one of those awful living museums. As we sit she makes tea and chats to Medhanie. They talk for a while as I look around the room. We are in the living area, which is pretty much empty apart from a couple of wooden poles which look as if they have held the place up for ever, some large clay pots, presumably for carrying water, various unidentifiable (at least by me) items hanging from the ceiling, and what looks like a tiny clay oven. Medhanie crouches in front of the oven thing and starts to show me how he used to grind the grain on its top when he was a young boy.

We sit for a while drinking tea and eating bread, and then a toddler comes stumbling into the room. A young woman rushes in after him, then sees our group and lets out a delighted squeal as she recognizes Medhanie and Mehawi. They kiss and then talk and then she kisses me and scoops up her toddler and brings him to kiss me. Two other children, both girls, are standing by the door, and she ushers them in and tells them to kiss me, which they do reluctantly before hiding behind one of the wooden poles.

'Does she live here?' I ask Medhanie.

'Yes, she was our neighbour,' he replies.

'Are the children hers?' I ask, not wanting it to sound like a criticism.

'Yes, they are all hers,' he says. 'She is the same age as you. If you had stayed you would have played together.' He then says something to her in Tigrinya, and she smiles and laughs and moves her hands between the two of us.

'Tell her her children are beautiful,' I say.

Medhanie tells her, to which she replies, via my brother, 'I thank God for my children, but you are lucky to escape, otherwise you would have ended up the same as me.'

This is the first time I don't feel angry when someone tells me how 'lucky' I was to be adopted. All I feel is sad because everyone in this room knows she's right.

'Hannah, you haven't seen the rest of the house yet,' says Medhanie, breaking the silence. 'Come, let me show you,' he says.

Nervously I follow him through a sort of arch that divides the back of the house from the front. 'This is the kitchen,' says Medhanie, pointing to a wall of intricate shelves built into the mud wall. More clay pots line the wall, and an *injera* pan and basket are on the stove. There is also a ledge with a small door (or a large window) that leads outside. Medhanie turns around and points to the other side of the room, which is separated off by a low wall. 'This is the bedroom, and this is the bed you were born on,' he says, spinning round grandly and then jumping up to sit on the bed as a finale.

I don't know what I had expected, or how I had expected to feel, but the numbness is back, and standing here it just doesn't feel real.

'Take a picture of me sitting on the bed,' says Medhanie.

I desperately don't want Medhanie to sense that I'm at all upset or freaked out by being here, so I'm relieved he's given me an excuse to look busy by rummaging in my bag for my camera and then taking his picture. And yet all the while I am doing this I'm fighting back both tears and the urge to run. I can feel myself getting cross with Medhanie for being so cheerful. I want to tell him it feels disrespectful to be taking pictures here, where our mother died, but then that's not the only thing this room represents to him. He has happy memories to outweigh the sad.

'And now I will take your picture on the bed,' he chirps, taking my camera before I have a chance to protest. I sit gingerly on the edge of the bed, feeling like one of those mawkish tourists who visit famous people's graves. The camera feels all wrong, salacious and macabre at the same time. Am I really going to sit around with friends at home and say, 'and this is me sitting on the bed where I was born and my mother died'? Exactly. And it's not as if I'll ever forget that I've been here, so why the need for photographic proof? Something else is wrong. With Medhanie here I can't relax, can't let whatever being in this room makes me feel come out, for fear of upsetting him. He will have grieved for his mother decades ago – who am I to stir that up again? Besides, compared to Medhanie, what right do I have to get upset? It's not as if I knew her, or ever got used to her being around. To Medhanie, to all of the others, she was a real person; to me she has only ever been a concept. Maybe that's why I'm uncomfortable with him in the room, because in this room there is no escaping the fact he has more of a claim to her than I ever could. She was his mother, she fed him, washed him, looked after him for years. If she even held me it will only have been for a few moments. I have no memories of her. The only real thing I know about my mother is that she died almost as soon as she gave birth to me, here, in this room, on this bed. There is no way to separate those facts. Had I not been born, Medhanie would be standing here with his mother, not a sister he barely knows. Is he thinking the same thing, wondering what he did to get such a rough deal, wishing he could trade me in to have his mother back? How was her sudden disappearance explained to him? Does he remember her death? Was he here in the *hidmo*, or had he been shooed away by elders who decided a delivery room was no place for a small boy? Did he return to find his mother gone? Did he even get a chance to say goodbye? Did he hate me when he realized I'd taken his mother away? How could he not blame me? I blame myself, even though I know there is nothing I could have done to save her – so somewhere, perhaps not even that deep inside, he must also blame me.

'Is it OK if I sit in here for a few more minutes?' I ask Medhanie as he hands me back the camera.

'Of course. I will wait for you in the living area,' he replies, stepping through the gap in the low wall.

When he is gone, I walk around the sleeping area, touching everything – the walls, the few clay storage pots that are on the floor (how old are they? did she carry them?) – and then finally I come back to the bed. I run my hand along it, noting how cleverly it is built into the walls of the *hidmo*, a solid mass, like a waist-high ledge. Double-checking that the others are engrossed in their conversation, I slip off my shoes and lie down on it – strange how just a few moments ago I was desperate to leave the room, and now I'm drawn to the bed. I look around the room, seeing what she would have seen. I close my eyes and take a deep breath, smelling what she would have smelt. And then, keeping my eyes closed, I lie there for a few moments, just listening out for the sounds she would have heard – the chatter in the living area, the chickens outside, and the occasional donkey. This is as close to her as I will ever get.

Worried about the others walking in on me, I open my eyes and sit back up. I sit there for a while longer, not sure what

I'm waiting for, and then the tears come. Not forced, not sobs, just a few tears at the sadness of it all. I will never meet my mother, I will never see a photograph of her, but at least I now have something to remember.

I take a couple more deep breaths to shake the melancholy feeling, and then go and join the others. Medhanie wants to show me where he used to play, so we say goodbye to the woman who now lives in our house, and then climb to the top of the village. He points out where friends and relatives used to live, and also the cemetery where our mother is buried. 'Do you want to go there?' he asks.

'No, it's fine, I don't need to – the house was enough,' I say.

'Are you ready to leave?' he says.

'Yes, I am ready, and thank you so much for bringing me here, Medhanie.'

And then we go back down to the front of the house where Mehawi is looking anxiously at his watch. We take a few more pictures of both of us sitting outside the house, and then we start our walk back to Timnit's village.

28

When we arrive at Timnit's three hours later, we are greeted as though we've been gone for days. A space is cleared for us under the canopy and we are told to sit down and rest. Within minutes someone comes out with *injera* and pumpkin stew, which Timnit has made especially for my return after Medhanie told her I couldn't eat meat. Elsewhere under the canopy two long lines of men are sitting with impossibly sharp knives, effortlessly filleting carcasses and chopping meat – either goat or beef. Every so often someone comes along and collects what they have cut up and disappears with it into another hut. It's like a production line and a wedding rehearsal dinner in one. The women are in the other huts, either preparing the cut meat, making *suwa* or ensuring there is a mountain of *injera* for tomorrow's wedding feast.

It is Timnit's eldest daughter, Shiebet, who is getting married. She is 'about eighteen' though I suspect nearer sixteen, possibly younger. And although she is young by my standards I know that in the villages many families marry their daughters off even younger, despite the government and aid agencies trying to encourage them to do otherwise.

Despite my newly acquired status as spinster aunt at this wedding, I have been looking forward to it for two reasons: I am looking forward to the attention being on someone else for a change and I am looking forward to learning what a traditional Eritrean wedding is like. Plus there is the added bonus that, weddings being the draw they are, there will be more family here than in any other place so far.

When I ask what time the wedding will be I am met with shrugs and blank looks. 'Whenever the groom's party arrive,' is all I get by way of clarification. Eventually I pin Medhanie down to something a little more specific: 'Today we will start to celebrate and dance long into the night. In the morning we will finish preparing the food, and then at some point in the day the groom's party will come from his village to collect his bride. Then there will be the ceremony and they will be married. We will eat together, and then the groom and his family will take the bride with them to her new village.'

Tired from all that walking, and keen not to miss anything tomorrow, I attempt to bail out of the dancing at around 1 a.m., and am met with a wall of protest from Timnit, Medhanie and the drummer. I hang in there for a few more dances, and eventually get to bed just after 3 a.m., falling asleep to the sound of the drum and the crackle of the stereo and loudspeaker that has somehow been rigged up to work outside. When I wake to go to the toilet a couple of hours later everything is quiet but for the rustling of various animals stirring.

I get up at around nine and decide to go for a stroll before everyone else wakes, as the idea of some time to myself is appealing. When I return, Medhanie is already up, and I sense he is angry that I went off on my own. Ignoring his sulking, I ask him what he thinks I should wear for the wedding. We settle on the floor-length denim skirt and long-sleeved flower-print white shirt. I twitter on about weddings in England and how no one but the bride is allowed to wear white. We share a couple of bread rolls and some cheese (which we brought with us as we weren't sure there'd be anything other than meat to eat in the village), and then we walk to the main house, which is already bustling with activity. People are either helping to prepare the food, sitting around chatting, or, for the most part, both. We are waiting for the groom and his wedding party to arrive. As the morning turns into the early afternoon I seem to be the only one getting restless, but then again I'm the only one who doesn't really know what's going on. Medhanie keeps disappearing to talk to people, so I decide to try and find my mother's sister, the one we met on the path yesterday. After a few minutes of searching (made harder because everywhere I go a swarm of children follows me) I spot her sitting in one of the few areas of shade (the canopy is now roasting). She jumps up and kisses me all over again. Then she grabs my hand and takes me over to a log where there are three other women, one of whom is the drummer from our first night here. One by one, the women start to cry and touch me – as if they can't believe their eyes. It's a much quieter crying than most I have experienced here, and their touches are much gentler. The drummer, the youngest of the four, is the only one who speaks English, but for once I know what is going on – they are all my mother's sisters. As they pull me down to join them on their log, the four of them carry on talking, each breaking off intermittently to either stroke my face (they already have hold of each hand) or my leg. It's all very understated, as if it's the most normal thing in the world for me to be sitting here with them, and yet at the same time they have to keep reminding themselves that it's real, and it's making me feel wonderful. I don't need to be taking part in the conversation to be included. I am happy just to be sitting here thinking, 'I am sitting with my mother's sisters.'

A while later, Medhanie comes running up the hill and tells us the groom's wedding party are on their way. There is a commotion as people rush to welcome them, and my aunts disappear into the main hut, presumably to tell Timnit, who must make sure her daughter, Shiebet, is safely inside.

At the head of the wedding party are five or six priests, and then comes the groom, surrounded by his best man and two other friends who will help him through the day. Behind them are the rest of the groom's party – his family, village elders, friends and so on. Everyone is singing and dancing, some are waving sticks, others their hands. As they come closer, our wedding party starts to sing in response to them, and once everyone is under the canopy we all dance together, until eventually our group breaks off and the visitors carry on. Then the dances take on a relay quality, with different groups – the elders, the women, the men, the children, etc. – taking it in turns to dance in a circle underneath the canopy. This goes on for about an hour until a young woman, the bride's best friend, comes out of the hut and whispers something to the best man. A hush descends and everyone sits down on the stools, chairs and logs that have been laid out. To the right is the 'top table' – a small table with six chairs around it, one each for the bride, groom, his best men and the bridesmaid. As the groom and his best man take their places behind the table, two older men from the groom's party then open up a suitcase full of women's clothes and show them around the circle to much appreciation.

'What is it?' I ask as Medhanie shoves me forwards, instructing me to take a picture of the suitcase.

'They are clothes the groom has bought his bride: they are new clothes for her new life,' he replies. I dutifully take a picture, but feel odd doing so, as if I am colluding with something rather unsavoury. I'm also acutely aware that not only am I one of only three people out of about a hundred with a camera, but I am also the only woman with one, and my camera is conspicuously small, shiny and new.

The suitcase disappears into the hut and the bridesmaid follows. After a while she comes out of the hut and whispers something to one of the best men. Then the two of them go into the hut.

'What's going on?' I ask Medhanie.

'The bride doesn't want to come out, she's too nervous,' he replies.

'But she's met him before, right?'

'No, of course not. It is an arranged marriage. The bride's and groom's parents have met, and Timnit has met the groom, but, no, the bride has not.'

'So she has never met the man she is about to marry?'

'That's right, she has never even seen him.'

'So we have seen the groom before she has?' I ask, astonished.

'That's right,' says Medhanie.

'But she's so much taller than him, what if she doesn't like short men?' I say, trying to make light of things, not wanting to offend Medhanie or the rest of the family on what is supposed to be a day of celebration. I am surprised by how shocked I am. I knew the wedding was arranged, but I didn't ever really stop to think what that meant – in this case a teenage girl (I'd say seventeen at the oldest) marrying a man who looks to be in his mid to late twenties (at least) whom she has never set eyes on. No wonder she doesn't want to come out of that hut. As people with concerned looks rush in and out of the hut, Medhanie tells me they are all trying to persuade the bride, my niece, to come out. A crazy thought of me joining them and then, once in there, secretly swapping places with her enters my head. She could be on a bus on the way to Asmara before anyone realizes she's gone, and I'd be safe – at twenty-nine I'm far too old for this man, and not exactly chaste. The best man is back, and he takes his place behind the table next to the groom. He says something to the groom, who nods. At first I think he looks relieved, but then I see a flicker of something else – could he be just as scared as his young bride? The groom then gets up and walks towards the hut. 'He is going to find his bride,' says Medhanie, preempting my question.

A quiet sense of expectation descends upon the crowd. All heads turn towards the entrance of the hut as the groom walks in. A couple of minutes go by, and then singing starts to come from the hut. Timnit and others are the first to come outside, and suddenly the place erupts as the singing turns into high-pitched celebratory shrilling and clapping. In the middle of the mêlée are the bride and groom, linked by their forefingers. She is wearing a traditional yellow-and-gold dress, her head is covered with the same fabric and she is wearing gold earrings (all of which I recognize from the suitcase). She looks breathtakingly beautiful, even though she has been crying.

They sit behind the table and the women bring food out. The bride and groom feed each other, to much cheering, and the party atmosphere returns. I'm unsure as to whether or not I've missed some sort of ceremony until Medhanie tells me that they are indeed now married. Everyone else then starts to eat. People are either drinking *suwa*, which I have been warned off for the sake of my stomach, or soft drinks (Coke or Fanta). This is the first wedding I've been to for a long time where I have been sober. After everyone has finished eating we all move around so that a group of men (the village elders) are sitting in the middle of the canopy facing another, smaller group of men.

'You will like this part: they are about to arrange the dowry,' says Medhanie.

But I don't like it; in fact I've gone off the whole wedding thing more and more as it has gone on. I feel as if I'm celebrating a young girl being taken from her family and friends in exchange for some cattle. Why would you celebrate this? Even as Medhanie tells me that she is allowed to have her best friend stay with her for the first few days in her new village, I can't shake the feeling that it's all wrong. Later, when Timnit tells me she is not sad to lose her daughter for she has ensured she is with a good man from a good family, I don't believe she means it. I know things are different here, I know I have to respect other people's traditions, but these aren't just 'other people', they are my family.

Later, when I'm back in Asmara, I tell one of my returnee friends how shocking I found the wedding. 'You must realize that in the villages having a husband, a good man, can be the difference between eating and not eating,' she tells me. 'To them, it is us who marry complete strangers.'

29

Medhanie and I leave Timnit's the morning after the wedding. Despite the fact I have eaten nothing more adventurous than pumpkin, *injera*, bread and cheese for four days, I have been throwing up and having diarrhoea through the night. The bus journey back is hellish, and I have to stop the bus twice to get off, the spectacularly low point being when, about half an hour out of Dersseney, I find myself crouched down in full view of the bus with diarrhoea coming out of one end and vomit the other. Eventually we make it back to Asmara, me fragile and grumpy but in one piece. Medhanie wants to take me to see a doctor, but I manage to persuade him to hold off until the morning, by which time I'm sure I'll be OK. I only have a couple of days left, and I don't want to spend them in a waiting room, and besides, I'm sure medical resources are stretched enough without a poor little rich girl who's probably just got a touch of traveller's tummy bothering them. As Medhanie drops me off at my hotel he makes me promise to call him if I get worse, and tells me he'll be over to check on me first thing. I can't be sure but I think he also tells the receptionist to keep an eye on me. Instead of feeling annoyed by his fussing, I find it touching. I have been a complete pain the last few hours, and yet he's carried on looking after me. Is this how big brothers behave?

I go straight to my room and collapse on the bed. It's as if my body was holding out until the last village trip before seizing up completely. I'd give anything to be in my own flat right now, or just to have my own toilet within reach. I drift off listening to the comfort blanket that is the World Service, dreaming of a hot bath.

I wake at about seven the next morning, thinking how typical it is that my body clock has finally adjusted and now I'm about to go home. Eritrea is only four hours ahead of England, but the routine – work tends to start at seven, lunch is from twelve to three, then there's work again until seven – is so different that I've been all over the place. When I arrived I was getting up just as everyone was having their lunchtime nap.

Thankfully, the sickness and diarrhoea have gone as quickly as they came, and in fact, I feel remarkably sprightly. I feel guilty admitting it, but I'm looking forward to going home. I feel my decision to fly with Lufthansa rather than Eritrean Airlines will pay off now, because as far as I'm concerned as soon as I step on to that plane I'm back in Europe. Medhanie and my cousin Hadish, who lives in Asmara and is the son of my now favourite Eritrean aunt, Rigbay, have offered to take me to the airport. Actually, they have insisted. I'm going to meet them for an early dinner tomorrow and leave straight afterwards. That means I've got today and tomorrow to do with as I please, so I've decided to spend the day revisiting my favourite places in Asmara and saying goodbye to some of the friends I've made.

I woke pleased I was going home soon, but now as I arrange to see people to say goodbye, I'm starting to wish I had a little more time. Without realizing it, I've made some real friends, and as time has gone on I've started to feel a part of something. I don't mean my birth family, but another family – one I hadn't expected to find.

When I arrived I deliberately made myself steer clear of the expat community, just because I thought it would be too easy to spend all my time with them. But the other community, the one I hadn't really bargained on but which has come to mean a lot to me, is the returnees – the Eritreans brought up in the West who have given up their old lives of relative luxury in exchange for constant dust, intermittent electricity and in some cases a stint of military service. They are neither expat nor local, but somewhere in between. Of course they are by definition better off than the average Eritrean, but they have made trying to do 'their bit', their life. They live surrounded by poverty, hunger and the ever-present threat of war. But it's not just the sacrifices they have made, material or otherwise, that have gotten under my skin, it's what they represent. Because of this country's bloody history, every family has someone who has been displaced. It may be a child given up for adoption, it may be sisters smuggled across the border to Sudan, it may be whole branches of the family tree living in asylum in Europe. That is who these returnees are. They don't speak Tigrinya, they can't cook *injera* and they don't dress right. Their skin colour means they never quite fitted in wherever they grew up, and their upbringing means they don't quite fit in here. In short, they are like me. It is this group of people who have been like an island of calm throughout my trip. For the duration of my stay here, I have felt most at home among them; I have felt the most me. And as I prepare to say my goodbyes, I wonder if it is this feeling that I have been searching for all along, and what it will be like, having finally found it, to leave that feeling behind.

I spend the day strolling up and down Liberation Avenue, meeting people in cafés, and marvelling at how used to this place I have become. I may be desperate to get back to my own life, but I have fallen in love with Asmara, so much so that I even experience that 'I'm home' feeling when I have been away for a few days. I loved the villages, and I adored Keren, but I love the ebb and flow of Asmara and, most importantly, I no longer feel like a tourist. Few would mistake me for anything other than a returnee (when someone does think I'm Asmarino born and bred it makes me feel giddy), but that's OK because what I've come to realize is that, different as they are, everyone agrees on one thing: returnees belong here. And that's what this new feeling, this new confidence, is. Finally, I feel as if I belong.

If you can't miss what you never had, was I better off before I came to Eritrea? Saying goodbye to Medhanie and Hadish is hard, mostly because I have no idea when I will see them again, or what happens now. What does it mean that I am sad to say goodbye to them, and yet a part of me is already on that plane, planning what drink I am going to order? I have to struggle not to run towards the gate, since I don't want them to think I am glad to be leaving, or that I haven't had a good time with them. I check in my bags and go to departures. I hand over my $20 for my departure tax. The man behind the counter eyes me suspiciously. He says something to me in Tigrinya.

'I'm sorry, I don't speak Tigrinya,' I say, hopefully.

'Where is your Eritrean ID card?' he barks.

'I don't have one,' I reply.

'Where were you born?' he asks.

'Keren,' I reply, for the first time enjoying the fact I can now picture what Keren looks like.

'Then you are Eritrean. You must have an ID. Until I see

your ID you cannot leave,' he says, flicking through my passport with disdain. He actually thinks I'm trying to skip the country.

I take a deep breath and, trying to hide the panic in my voice with annoyance, I reply, 'I don't have one. This is my first time here. I was adopted, I am a British citizen – look, you have my passport right there.'

'Adopted? What is this "adopted"?'

'Adopted – put in an orphanage and then found new parents.'

'White people?' the man grunts, as if he could imagine no worse fate.

'Yes, white people, that's right,' I reply, pleased I seem to have finally got through to him, albeit in a rather simplistic way.

'Ah, OK, I understand,' he says, his tone softening, but only slightly. 'Next time you come here you must get an Eritrean ID. And you must learn Tigrinya, you are one of us,' he says, and then smiles as he hands me back my passport. I walk up the stairs, relieved and amused: that is the first time I have ever had problems *leaving* a country.

30

I have been back in London for two days. I have not seen or spoken to anyone. I am about to start telling the world I am back, but I just need some time on my own before all the questions start. True to form, as soon as I sat down on the plane I started wondering if perhaps I should have stayed a little longer. As we were flying over Jordan I suddenly found it impossible to remember everyone's faces. My father was the hardest, then Timnit. Since my return the whole trip has taken on a dreamlike quality. Did I really just get on a plane to Eritrea and meet my father? Was it me who didn't make a fuss about my recently pedicured feet having to walk over animal bones to go to the toilet? Could I have ever slept outside listening to hyenas? It's my time in the villages especially that I can't quite get over. That was when I felt I really got to know people, got closest to whatever it was I went looking for. All my life I have assumed I would feel 'right' if only I met my birth family. I talked about meeting my birth family with the same desire other people talked about meeting their soulmate. I have argued in favour of that cliché about the missing jigsaw piece. And now I have finally put my money where my mouth is: I have shared meals with my father and jokes with my sister. I have met my mother's family and her best friend. I have become the youngest of six, or the middle child of thirteen if you include my half-siblings. I am also now an aunt to thirteen new nephews and nieces. And to think I grew up thinking I was an orphan.

So why can't I leave the house? Why aren't I out there telling everyone how wonderful it all is? The short answer is that I'm tired: tired from the travelling, from the constant having to be nice, from being sick while I was out there. The honest answer is that I don't want to see anyone because I don't think I can cope with other people right now. I've got all this stuff, all these new people, swimming around in my head and I worry that if people start asking me questions I'll either combust or dissolve with the head-fuck of it all.

And so I spend two days (three nights if you include the night I got back) locked away in my flat, trying to find room inside my head for all these new people, trying to figure out how the hell I feel. After a couple of days friends start leaving chirpy messages on my answerphone, but this just makes me feel even more disorientated. Life seems to have carried on, and even though I've been through so much, friends are calling casually, just as they did before, to see if I fancy 'a quick drink after work'. Nothing has changed and yet everything is different. I try to stop obsessing about how surreal everything has become – both Eritrea and, now I'm back, London or at least the London that's outside my flat. I just can't seem to focus. The smallest of things, such as restocking my fridge, take on massive significance. I venture out to the supermarket but am so dazed by the experience that I just grab a packet of pasta, some fruit and some bread and then leave. It is only when I empty the shopping bag that I realize that what I have bought is what I ate for a good chunk of my trip – if they'd sold *injera* and *shiro* would I have come out with that?

I hope I don't turn into one of those annoying travel bores – you know, the ones who return from a fortnight in India harping on about the plight of the starving millions as if they'd only just realized they exist. What if my life suddenly offends me? And if it doesn't, perhaps it should? It is one thing to spend a fortune on shoes and bags without a second thought, it is quite another to do so when you know your sister and her family would not survive without food aid. I found it hard enough to read or see reports of drought, potential famine and possible war before I went to Eritrea, so what will it be like now I can put names and faces to the statistics? As long as I stay here, alone in my flat, I won't have to deal with any of those things, or answer any of those questions.

Except of course I will. I could stay here for weeks, months, a year and still those questions, and plenty more, would plague me, because it's not other people's thoughts about my trip I can't escape, it's my own. After the initial high of being surrounded by my own things again I seem to have come crashing down and am either crying, on the verge of crying, or washing my face after crying. That's another reason I'm not that keen to go out. Sometimes it's just a little cry, a sort of 'everything feels so hopeless' cry, other times I find myself sobbing.

The first person I call is my dad. He rang the day I got back but my head was still in bits – instead of picking up the telephone I burst into tears when I heard his voice on the machine; I desperately wanted to pick it up but for some reason just couldn't. I can hear the relief in my dad's voice immediately. 'You're back,' he sighs. 'How did it go – the meeting, everything? Are you OK?'

Epilogue

This time last year I was sunbathing on my balcony in Asmara. I thought it was my last free day before I met my family, but actually, I was about to get a call telling me to be ready in ten minutes. By the kind of startling coincidence that only happens in real life, a very close friend is meeting her birth mother for the first time today. The combination of seeing someone else try to prepare herself for something similar to what I went through and my own anniversary has knocked me for six.

When I came back from Eritrea I retreated from my normal life. I spent a lot of time on my own, avoiding other people because I knew they would want me to talk about my trip, which was something I couldn't face. It took me weeks to get the photographs developed, and another couple of weeks before I could look at them; they just sat in a corner of my flat, unopened. When I did eventually open them I was fine looking at the first roll – Liberation Avenue, pictures of that wonderful first afternoon with Teame – but as soon as I got to the first picture of me meeting my family I burst into tears, as if the emotion I couldn't summon up then had been transposed on to the photographs. I still find those pictures hard to look at – I can see that I am smiling and giving off the right signals, but I also remember just how freaked out I felt in that room.

It is only now that I can see irony in the fact that other

people were desperate to see my photographs when I could barely look at them, much less have other people pore over them as if they were regular holiday snaps.

I pretty much stopped going out, instead spending my evenings and weekends locked away inside my own head. Reading, my usual refuge, ceased to be an escape because I already felt I had too many new characters in my life to have the energy to focus on yet more. Instead I went to the cinema, rented videos and watched endless hours of television – anything as long as it wasn't too taxing but was distracting enough to make me at least have a stab at pretending I wasn't thinking about everything I'd just done. My head was a mess. When I wasn't feeling guilty about the way I lived compared to the way my family did, I was feeling angry at them for having given me up in the first place, for the family life I had missed out on but had now caught a glimpse of. It became easier to not see friends than to have to try and explain my emotions. As the months passed, I lost quite a few friends. Some took it personally that I wouldn't talk to them about my trip, as if I owed it to the friendship, to them. At first I tried to spill as they wanted me to, but I ended up either angry at them for asking what I saw as stupid questions, or angry at myself for reducing the biggest moment of my life into some sort of after-dinner performance. Don't get me wrong, I was very good at it – just the right number of jokes, lowering my voice to a whisper to make them feel special, gazing into the middle distance during the silences to give the illusion of sadness. But that wasn't ever enough. People either felt cheated that I didn't honour them by crying on their shoulder, or they got so freaked out by the magnitude of it all that they broke down themselves. I got just as angry with both camps. Those who kept prodding me to see if I was human, who tried to break through my practised routine, were rewarded with jokes and assurances that I was fine; really, it was all a walk in the park. And the criers, well, I'd put my arm around them, but inside I'd be raging and thinking, 'If I can manage not to cry, how dare you?'

But it was never what my friends would think that I worried about when I planned this trip, it was what my dad would think, and what it would do to our relationship, that I agonized over. It was months before I could be honest with him about Eritrea, before I told him just how hard it was, and how I really felt meeting my father. I was paranoid about hurting him, about making him feel surplus to requirements somehow. I couldn't show my dad photographs of my father for over six months – pretending that I'd forgotten to bring them with me each time I saw him. But, as ever, while I tied myself up in knots, my dad played the long game. He was patient, didn't pressurize me to talk too deeply, and let me know he'd be there when I was ready. Eventually, it all came out, even the part about me worrying I'd end up losing him: 'You're my daughter, Hannah,' he said, 'no matter what you do.'

Tom and Lydia were also completely unfazed by my trip, and the fact I now have four other siblings. The idea that they'd mean any less to me, or I to them, simply hasn't occurred to them, or if it has they've immediately dismissed it. I don't think I could love them any more or be prouder of how they've dealt with the whole thing if they were my own children. They've both said they'd like to come with me on my next trip to Eritrea. Imagine that – both my families in one place! I haven't booked my next trip, but one is definitely on the cards. I think I'd like to go once a year, maybe even try and live there for a few months, once I've learnt the language. I catch myself missing the vibe of Asmara, and the feeling of lightness as I walked down Liberation Avenue. Tsehainesh, Nebiat and a couple of other returnee friends have passed through London in the last year, and each time I see them I miss the others, and Eritrea, even more. And then, of course, there is my family. It feels silly saying I miss people I have only just met, but it's true – they feel so far away. My father, Timnit and Stephanos feel the furthest: how do you have a long-distance relationship with someone who doesn't speak the same language? Keeping in touch has fallen to Medhanie and Zemichael, who have been fantastic e-mail correspondents and invaluable help with the writing of this book. I have grown so incredibly fond of them both that it won't be long before I won't remember what life was like without them. Not long after I returned to London, Medhanie sent me a photograph of Himan, my sister who died on the front. Everyone was right: I do look like her.

A friend asked me the other day if I regretted going to Eritrea, opening the can. I don't. But I do wish I'd known then what I know now. Finding my birth family was the easiest bit. OK, it wasn't exactly a relaxing break, but it was a breeze compared with trying to figure out where we go from now.

He just wanted a decent book to read ...

Not too much to ask, is it? It was in 1935 when Allen Lane, Managing Director of Bodley Head Publishers, stood on a platform at Exeter railway station looking for something good to read on his journey back to London. His choice was limited to popular magazines and poor-quality paperbacks – the same choice faced every day by the vast majority of readers, few of whom could afford hardbacks. Lane's disappointment and subsequent anger at the range of books generally available led him to found a company – and change the world.

'We believed in the existence in this country of a vast reading public for intelligent books at a low price, and staked everything on it'
Sir Allen Lane, 1902–1970, founder of Penguin Books

The quality paperback had arrived – and not just in bookshops. Lane was adamant that his Penguins should appear in chain stores and tobacconists, and should cost no more than a packet of cigarettes.

Reading habits (and cigarette prices) have changed since 1935, but Penguin still believes in publishing the best books for everybody to enjoy. We still believe that good design costs no more than bad design, and we still believe that quality books published passionately and responsibly make the world a better place.

So wherever you see the little bird – whether it's on a piece of prize-winning literary fiction or a celebrity autobiography, political tour de force or historical masterpiece, a serial-killer thriller, reference book, world classic or a piece of pure escapism – you can bet that it represents the very best that the genre has to offer.

Whatever you like to read – trust Penguin.